$28.70

The Comanche

Tom Streissguth

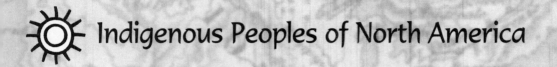
The Comanche

Tom Streissguth

Lucent Books, Inc.
P.O. Box 289011, San Diego, California

Titles in the Indigenous Peoples of North America Series Include:

The Apache
The Cherokee
The Comanche
The Iroquois
Native Americans of the Great Lakes
Native Americans of the Northeast
Native Americans of the Plains
Native Americans of the Southeast
Native Americans of the Southwest
The Navajo
The Sioux

Library of Congress Cataloging-in-Publication Data

Streissguth, Thomas, 1958–
   The Comanche / by Tom Streissguth.
       p. cm. — (Indigenous peoples of North America)
Includes bibliographical references and index.
Summary: A history of this Indian tribe of the Southern Plains and a
description of their customs, religion, relationship with other tribes, and
twentieth-century changes to their traditional way of life.
   ISBN 1-56006-633-4
   1. Comanche Indians—Juvenile literature. [1. Comanche Indians. 2.
Indians of North America—Great Plains. 3. Indians of North America—
Southwest, New.] I. Title. II. Series.
   E99.C85 S77 2000
   978'.0049745—dc21
                                                                99-050594

Copyright 2000 by Lucent Books, Inc.
P.O. Box 289011, San Diego, California 92198-9011

Printed in the U.S.A.

Contents

Foreword

North America's native peoples are often relegated to history—viewed primarily as remnants of another era—or cast in the stereotypical images long found in popular entertainment and even literature. Efforts to characterize Native Americans typically result in idealized portrayals of spiritualists communing with nature or bigoted descriptions of savages incapable of living in civilized society. Lost in these unfortunate images is the rich variety of customs, beliefs, and values that comprised—and still comprise—many of North America's native populations.

The *Indigenous Peoples of North America* series strives to present a complex, realistic picture of the many and varied Native American cultures. Each book in the series offers historical perspectives as well as a view of contemporary life of individual tribes and tribes that share a common region. The series examines traditional family life, spirituality, interaction with other native and non-native peoples, warfare, and the ways the environment shaped the lives and cultures of North America's indigenous populations. Each book ends with a discussion of life today for the Native Americans of a given region or tribe.

In any discussion of the Native American experience, there are bound to be sim-

ilarities. All tribes share a past filled with unceasing white expansion and resistance that led to more than four hundred years of conflict. One U.S. administration after another pursued this goal and fought Indians who attempted to defend their homelands and ways of life. Although no war was ever formally declared, the U.S. policy of conquest precluded any chance of white and Native American peoples living together peacefully. Between 1780 and 1890, Americans killed hundreds of thousands of Indians and wiped out whole tribes.

The Indians lost the fight for their land and ways of life, though not for lack of bravery, skill, or a sense of purpose. They simply could not contend with the overwhelming numbers of whites arriving from Europe or the superior weapons they brought with them. Lack of unity also contributed to the defeat of the Native Americans. For most, tribal identity was more important than racial identity. This loyalty left the Indians at a distinct disadvantage. Whites had a strong racial identity and they fought alongside each other even when there was disagreement because they shared a racial destiny.

Although all Native Americans share this tragic history they have many distinct differences. For example, some tribes and individuals sought to cooperate almost immediately with the U.S. government while others steadfastly resisted the white presence. Life before the arrival of white settlers also varied. The nomads of the Plains developed altogether different lifestyles and customs from the fishermen of the Northwest coast.

Contemporary life is no different in this regard. Many Native Americans—forced onto reservations by the American government—struggle with poverty, poor health, and inferior schooling. But others have regained a sense of pride in themselves and their heritage, enabling them to search out new routes to self-sufficiency and prosperity.

The *Indigenous Peoples of North America* series attempts to capture the differences as well as similarities that make up the experiences of North America's native populations—both past and present. Fully documented primary and secondary source quotations enliven the text. Sidebars highlight events, personalities, and traditions. Bibliographies provide readers with ideas for further research. In all, each book in this dynamic series provides students with a wealth of information as well as launching points for further research.

The Comanche and the Southern Plains

The southern Great Plains of North America extend from New Mexico and Colorado east along the Red, Arkansas, Canadian, and other shallow tributaries of the Mississippi River. To the south, the Rio Grande divides the plains country from the deserts of northern Mexico. The climate throughout the southern plains is dry, with mild winters and hot summers. In winter, bitterly cold blizzards may strike. In spring and summer, violent thunderstorms often roll across the landscape, bringing rain, hail, and tornadoes.

For the most part, the southern plains are treeless. Deep-rooted prairie grasses cover the ground, with scattered cottonwood, oak, and elm trees growing along the rivers. The land stretches to the horizon in a series of low hills; in few places is the terrain completely flat. The Indians who lived here used the rivers as their highways, navigating by familiar buttes, hills, and cliffs. Escarpments, or broken, low cliff faces, rise in many places around the headwaters of the major rivers. These provided springs of fresh water, grass for horses, and shelter from the cold winds of winter.

The Comanche arrived in this area in the late seventeenth century, after a long migration from the mountains and basins of the northern Rocky Mountains. For two centuries, they roamed all over the southern plains, hunting and fighting in a region that outsiders called the Comancheria. By the mid–nineteenth century, however, the Comanche saw their claim to this land challenged by American settlers determined to drive them from their hunting grounds. When pressed by the superior arms and greater numbers of the white settlers, a small band of determined warriors retreated into the high tablelands known as the Llano Escatado, or Staked Plain. Here, in a harsh and waterless area that demanded the highest survival skills, the Comanche nation made a last stand for its traditional life on the plains.

A Challenging Environment

Until the late nineteenth century, the Comancheria was no place for outsiders, and any stranger seeking to enter or cross this land did so at great risk. Permanent settlement in the region was difficult; even today the towns are scattered and small, the ranches many miles apart. Rainfall is scarce, and periodic droughts turn the topsoil into great clouds of dust. The last severe drought on the southern plains, in the 1930s, put an end to the Comanche's agricultural efforts on their reservation. The land was fruitful in the early days, however, and in certain seasons, Comanche women could gather a fine harvest of edible roots and berries, plums, wild grapes, walnuts, and persimmons.

In fact, until the arrival of white settlers and hunters, wildlife was abundant. Deer, elk, antelope, and huge herds of bison flourished on the thick prairie grasses of the region. According to one historian,

The number of buffalo on the plains before commercial slaughter began reached a figure that staggers the imagination. In Kansas alone, it has been estimated that the bones of thirty-one million head were gathered and sold for fertilizer between 1868 and 1881. A vast herd comprising con-

siderably more than four million animals was seen by competent witnesses in 1871 on the Arkansas River between Fort Zarah and Fort Larned. The main herd was fifty miles deep and twenty-five miles wide.[1]

This abundance of game on the Great Plains has been cited by some historians as

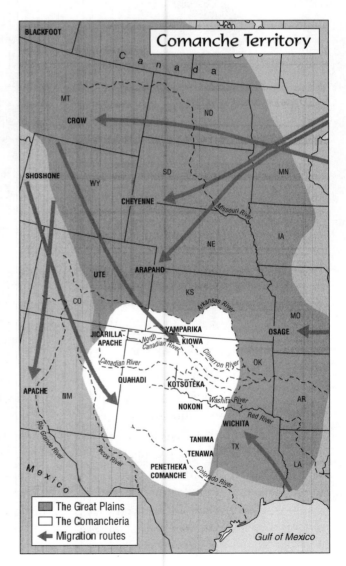

The Great Plains
The Comancheria
Migration routes

Game such as bison (pictured) flourished on the Great Plains before the arrival of white settlers and hunters.

one reason why the Comanche migrated to the area from their former home in the Rocky Mountains.

The Comanche Arrive on the Plains

The Comanche once belonged to the Shoshonean people, who lived mainly in what is now Colorado, Wyoming, southern Montana, and eastern Idaho. At the end of the seventeenth century, a large group of Shoshone began a migration down to the plains, first settling around the headwaters of the Arkansas River in eastern Colorado. Over the years, they gradually moved east and south, into eastern New Mexico, Texas, and Oklahoma.

Historians have offered several possible explanations for this migration, which resulted in the Comanche's identification as a people separate from the Shoshone. According to one theory, the Comanche were forced from their ancient home by rival bands in the late seventeenth century, when the Blackfeet were moving south and the Crow were moving west into northern Wyoming and into the land of the Shoshone. Another theory claims that, at the time of the migration, antelope, deer, bison, and other game were growing scarce in the mountain valleys of Colorado and Wyoming, causing many tribes to face starvation every winter. The plains, by contrast, offered abundant herds of game year-round, providing not only a surplus of food but also material for homes, clothing, and many different kinds of household goods. One student of Comanche history, Professor R. N. Richardson, writes, "I do not believe the Comanches were driven into the country. On the contrary, it seems they visited it, found that it was well suited to their mode of existence, and proceeded to fight for it and take it."[2]

The Comanche also may have been in search of horses, knowing that their new home on the plains demanded the mobility that horses provided. The horse had been brought to the region by Spanish settlers from New Spain (now Mexico). The Comanche soon learned that acquiring horses on the plains was much easier than finding them in the mountains, where the animals were still rare and the goods needed to trade for them even scarcer.

During their migration, the Comanche encountered something else that was entirely new to them. According to historian William T. Hagan, "It was on the southwestern edge of the plains that the Comanches had first seen white men—Spaniards from the settlements along the upper Rio Grande."[3]

Legends of the Migration

The Comanche have many different stories of their own to explain their migration. One of these stories claims that the Comanche split from the rest of the Shoshone after a fight between members of the two groups; another describes a bitter argument over a bear killed in a hunt.

A Comanche named Post Oak Jim gave the following account in 1933:

Two bands were living together in a large camp. One band was on the east side; the other on the west. Each had its own chief.

Every night the young boys were out playing games—racing, and so forth. They were having a kicking game; they kicked each other. One boy kicked another over the stomach so hard that he died from it. That boy who was killed was from the West camp. He was the son of a chief.

When this thing happened, the West camp cried all night. In the East camp, it was silent. Next day, they buried that boy.

The boy's father, the chief, had his crier go around announcing that there would be a big fight to see which camp was best so as to settle the question of his son's death. . . .

The two sides lined up, and the chiefs met in the center. Then an old man from the East camp came up into the center. He wept and told them it wasn't right for them to fight among themselves like that. . . .

11

The chief called it off. After that, the chief had his announcer tell the people it was time to move camp. "We have bad luck here. There has been hard feeling.". . .

Then they broke up. One group went north; those are the Shoshones. The other group went west.[4]

Whatever the motives behind their migration, the Comanche who had arrived on the southern plains were there to stay. The new conditions under which they lived, hunted, and raided shaped an entirely new lifestyle for the tribe, one they would maintain under difficult circumstances for the next two hundred years.

Chapter 1

First Encounters

The Comanche who moved down to the plains called themselves "the people," using a word in their own language that historians have spelled in different ways, including *numinuh, nimma, nermemah,* and *nummunuh.* In 1724, when the French explorer Etienne de Bourgemond came across several Comanche villages along the Kansas River, the Comanche homeland lay between the upper Platte and the

Meriwether Louis and William Clark, seen here with their guide, Sacajawea, explored along the Missouri River to the north.

headwaters of the Kansas River, on the western edge of the Great Plains. Eighty years later, during their exploration along the Missouri River to the north, Meriwether Lewis and William Clark heard of a vanished tribe whom the Sioux called the "Padouca." According to Lewis and Clark, the Padouca

occupied the country between the upper parts of the River Platte and the river Kanzas [and] were visited by Bourgemon[d] in 1724, and then lived on the Kanzas river. The seats [villages], which he describes as their residence, are now occupied by the Kanzas nation; and of the Padou-

cas there does not now exist even the name.[5]

In fact, the Padouca were the Comanche. By the time of Lewis and Clark's expedition, they had moved even farther south, into their future home south of the Canadian River. They quickly displayed an aggressive attitude toward Native American people of other tribes, with whom they now competed for the available wood, water, and hunting grounds on the southern plains. Indeed, the Comanche became rivals or outright foes of several different tribes, including the Cheyenne, the Arapaho, and the Sioux, who lived along the

Comanche History in One Paragraph

In 1911, the Encyclopedia Britannica briefly summed up the life and history of the Comanche with this short article.

"Comanches, a tribe of North American Indians of Shoshonean stock, so called by the Spaniards, but known to the French as Padoucas, an adaptation of their Sioux name, and among themselves as nimenim (people). They number some 1400, attached to the Kiowa agency, Oklahoma. When first met by Europeans, they occupied the regions between the upper waters of the Brazos and Colorado on the one hand, and the Arkansas and Missouri on the other. Until their final surrender in 1875 the Comanches were the terror of the Mexican and Texan frontiers, and were always famed for their bravery. They were brought to nominal submission in 1783 by the Spanish general Anza, who killed thirty of their chiefs. During the 19th century they were always raiding and fighting, but in 1867, to the number of 2500, they agreed to go on a reservation. In 1872 a portion of the tribe, the Quanhada or Staked Plains Comanches, had again to be reduced by military measures."

southern tributaries of the Missouri River. As the Comanche continued to move south, they also began fighting and raiding the Apache, the Kiowa, and the Wichita.

The Comanche had their longest conflict with the Ute tribe. At one time, the Comanche and Utes had joined together in raids on Spanish settlements and Pueblo Indian towns in New Mexico. By 1730, however, this friendship had turned to rivalry. The two tribes fought over territory around the Pecos River and the Rio Grande; the Comanche raided Ute horse herds and began driving their newfound foes westward. The Comanche became the principal enemy of the Ute, who stopped using the name *komantcia* (meaning enemy or stranger) for other unfriendly tribes and began applying it solely to the Comanche. This Ute word was later adopted by the Spanish in their colonial records, in which the new arrivals from the north were called the Comantcia. The term "enemy" probably seemed appropriate to the Spaniards because at this time the Comanche were constantly raiding their settlements for horses and captives.

The Comanche Bands

Every person who belonged to the Comanche tribe also belonged to a band. The Comanche bands date back to when the Comanche lived among the other Shoshonean people of the northern Rocky Mountains. The dry basins and steep mountains of the region could not support large groups of people, so the Comanche divided themselves into smaller communities. Over the years, each band came to identify itself with a name of its own, including the Penetheka (Honey Eaters), the Quahadi (Antelopes), the Hois (Timber People), the Parkeenaum (Water People), the Tenawa (People Who Live Downstream), and the Widyunu (Awl People).

When the Comanche moved down from the mountains and high basins and spread out over a much greater territory, the bands continued to go their separate ways. Made up of several different villages or camps, the bands moved constantly in their favored area. They followed the bison herds or moved whenever the grass, water, and game looked more promising elsewhere. They could split up and disappear or remain in one location for many generations and for as long as the members of the band and their elders could remember. Individual members of a band also might leave on their own to join a different group.

Each band depended on its own members for food and for protection from enemies. Each had a certain way of building homes, preparing campsites, dancing, preparing food, and communicating with the spirit world. Certain characteristics identified the band to the outside world and might also serve as its nickname. One band that often moved, for example, was known as the Nokoni, or "Wanderers."

Within each band, groups of related families lived together. The Comanche family groups were independent; each clan took responsibility for its own members. Each of the groups had a headman or chief. All the headmen of the band formed a council that gathered, when necessary, to make important decisions. Under certain circumstances, such as the outbreak of war against a rival tribe or during the annual bison hunt, a single leader was chosen. Very few Comanche ever rose to the position of permanent chief. Even when they did, their authority was limited—very few chiefs made important personal decisions for the members of their band or village.

Important Comanche Bands

In the nineteenth century, when the Comanche reached the height of their power in the southern plains, many of the smaller bands disappeared. Conditions had changed on the plains: Larger groups could raid and hunt more successfully, whereas smaller groups often suffered hunger and poverty. Gradually, the entire tribe divided itself into a few major bands. This division has lasted down to the present day. Most Comanche still identify themselves as members of one of five bands: the Penetheka, the Quahadi, the Yamparika, the Nokoni, and the Kotsoteka.

The Penetheka, whose name means Honey Eaters, were also known as the Wasps. The largest of all the Comanche bands, they led the tribe's migration across the Red River and into the Cross Timbers area of what is now Texas. Eventually they settled the farthest south of all the Comanche bands. According to their own tradition, the Penetheka moved so far away that for a time they lost contact with the rest of the Comanche bands entirely. After being found again by members of the Quahadi and Yamparika, who were riding south on a raid into Mexico, the Penetheka rejoined the Comanche.

In the twentieth century, the Penetheka lived on the southern half of the Comanche reservation, between the Red River and the Oklahoma town of Lawton. They were not only the band that first made contact with settlers coming west from the United States but also the first group to accept white ways. They were among the first to cease raiding on white settlements and among the first of the Comanche to live on a reservation. On occasion, the Penetheka even fought alongside the U.S. Army during its campaigns on the plains. On the divide between "progressive" and "traditional" that still exists among North American Indians, the Penetheka represent the "progressive" faction of the Comanche.

At the time of the great Comanche migration, the Quahadi, or Antelopes, moved with the Yamparika band into the dry and harsh Staked Plain. Among the white settlers, these "western Comanche" had the reputation of being the fiercest of all Comanche raiders, and the Quahadi would be among the last to settle on the reservation set out for them by the United States. After the Medicine Lodge Treaty of 1867, the Antelopes continued to battle the white soldiers for several years under the leadership of Chief Quanah Parker, the most famous among them and the best-known Comanche in history. Even after their traditional Comanche life came to an end, the Quahadi would not leave their traditional homes; many of them lived in tepees well into the twentieth century.

A Penetheka grips his bow. The Penetheka were the first Comanche band to accept the culture of white settlers

The Yamparika, or Yapai, were named after a favorite food—the root known as "yap," which they dug from the ground as the Shoshonean tribes of the northern mountains did. The Yamparika kept the Shoshonean traditions the longest, and among the Shoshone themselves all Comanche people were known as Yamparika. According to tradition, the Yamparika were the last Comanche band to break away from the mountains and migrate into the plains, where they finally settled between the Canadian and Arkansas Rivers, farther north than any other Comanche band.

A division still exists between the "northern" Comanche, including the Yamparika, and the southern Comanche, including the Penetheka. As described by anthropologist David Jones,

The Names of Others

In the late nineteenth and early twentieth centuries, ethnologist James Mooney spent much of his time among the Native American tribes of the Great Plains, studying their history, traditions, and languages. Mooney considered himself a scientist, and he was most interested in gathering and organizing data. The books and papers he wrote provide some of the richest information on Native Americans during their wrenching transition to reservation life. In his book *The Ghost-Dance Religion and the Sioux Outbreak of 1890*, Mooney devotes chapters to each of the tribes he studied as well as to tribal vocabularies. The following, according to Mooney, are the names the Comanche gave to tribes they encountered on the plains.

Saretika (Dog Eaters): Arapaho

Nashonit: Caddo

Paganavo (Striped Arrows): Cheyenne

Papitsinima (beheaders): Sioux

Taivo (Easterners): whites

Dokana (Tattooed People): Wichita

The following are some names that other tribes gave the Comanche.

Kiowa: Bodalkinago (Reptile People) or Gyaiko

Arapaho: Chatha (Enemies)

Kiowa Apache: Idahi (meaning unknown)

Navaho: Nalani (Many Enemies)

Wichita: Nataa (Snakes or Enemies)

Caddo: Sauhto (Snakes)

Cheyenne: Shishinowits-Itaniuw (Snake People)

Shoshone: Yampaini (Yap Eaters)

Osage, Kansa, and others: Padouca

A Comanche travels on his horse.

[Southern Comanches] are often referred to [by northern Comanches] in English as "Freckles," alluding to the great degree of mixed-blood Comanches who, the northerners believe, fill the southerner's ranks. The southern Comanches are less colorful than northerners in their invectives, simply stating that northerners are, for the most part, uneducated, drunken, shiftless, and generally responsible for the poor reputation which the Comanches possess in many of the white communities in southern Oklahoma.[6]

According to different sources, the name of the Nokoni means "Those Who Turn Back," "Those Who Move Often," or simply "Wanderers." The Nokoni had a reputation as being the most restless of the Comanche bands, moving from one camp to the next in search of better shelter or hunting. They ranged all over Texas between the Pecos River, in the western deserts, and the Red River, which forms part of the modern boundary between Texas and Oklahoma. According to historian James Mooney, the name *Nokoni* was forbidden among the Comanche after the death of Nokoni, the father of the famous Comanche chief Quanah Parker. After this event, the band was called the Detsanayuka, or Bad Campers, because they never settled long in one place.

The Nokoni shared their range with other, smaller bands such as the Tanima (Liver Eaters) and the Kotsoteka (Bison Eaters), who were among the ablest bison hunters of the Comanche. The Kotsoteka lived and roamed in the heart of bison country along and south of the Canadian River. From an early time, they traded and dealt with the comancheros, the Spanish traders and ranchers who lived in eastern New Mexico.

The Kotsoteka and the other bands usually kept good relations with these foreigners, especially after an important treaty was signed in 1786. The Spanish were never strong enough to lay claim to any land or hunting grounds the Comanche called their own. But the appearance of a new kind of white man, coming from the east and speaking English, put the Comanche on a collision course with a group of settlers who would put an end to their traditional way of life.

A Clash of Cultures

As white settlement in Texas increased in the 1830s and 1840s, the Comanche found themselves confronting people who lived in an entirely different manner, as permanent settlers on privately owned land. According to ethnologist James Mooney, "They were friendly to the Americans generally, but became bitter enemies of the Texans, by whom they were dispossessed of their best hunting grounds, and carried on a relentless war against them for nearly forty years."[7]

A group of Native American hunters attack a herd of bison. Despite repeated military campaigns in the Comancheria, the Spanish failed to occupy or control Comanche hunting grounds.

The settlers of Texas were pushing into the plains between the Rio Grande and the Red River, bringing their horses, wagons, farming tools, and weapons. They claimed plots of land near rivers and creeksides, where freshwater and grass were more plentiful. They built houses of wood or sod and, when they could, raised fences around their claims to corral livestock and to keep out strangers. They had no intention of moving by the season, as the Comanche and other Indian tribes did. Their homes were permanent, and they claimed the land—the grass, trees, rocks, and water—as their private possessions to be held by their families and no one else. Those strangers who crossed it, hunted on it, or otherwise tried to use it in any way were treated as enemies.

According to anthropologist David E. Jones,

By the early nineteenth century the bison herds were greatly diminished on the south Plains, and the Comanches increasingly turned to raiding to augment their economy. During this period the Comanches raided New Mexico, the Santa Fe Trail, northern Texas, and Old Mexico, sometimes as far south as Durango. Their greatest source of irritation during this span of

New Blood

Many Comanche historians have given different explanations for why the Comanche came to dominate such a vast region of the southern Great Plains in such a short time. The Comanche adopted the horse, for example, but many tribes had horses by the late eighteenth century. The Comanche were skilled fighters, but so were the Osage, Cheyenne, and Apache, all of whom the Comanche dominated south of the Canadian River. In their book *The Comanche People*, Joseph H. Cash and Gerald Wolff offer one more theory: By bringing captives of different backgrounds into their villages and families, the Comanche kept their nation vigorous and open to unfamiliar ways that often proved advantageous.

"Because of their small numbers, the Comanche willingly accepted new members in their bands. The only qualification was that the person had to be a Comanche or someone adopted into the tribe at one time or another. The Comanche, in an effort to keep up tribal membership, took many captives—particularly women and children—whom they adopted into the tribe. The women became the mothers of future Comanche warriors, while the children were trained as members of the tribe. The Comanche assimilated not only Indians but also Mexican and American captives. As a result, they developed a people with the vigor of the hybrid and acquired the numerous qualities and bits of knowledge contributed by those who came from different settings. This was unquestionably one of their greatest assets and helped them rise to the top. Certainly, there was no predetermined reason why the Comanche should have had any greater chance to dominate their area than any of the dozen other tribes."

time was the growing white settlements of Texas. It was during this period of increased contact with Texas that the division of the Comanche bands into northern, middle, western, and southern began to acquire a new meaning—one couched in terms of degree of acculturation and the hostilities engendered between the tradition-oriented and conservative Comanche bands and the well-acculturated Comanche bands.[8]

The Comanche were soon raiding the settlers' isolated homes and ranches, many of which were built at great distances from the white villages. The settlers defended themselves as best they

White settlers attempt to defend their house during a Native American raid. Comanche raids escalated during the nineteenth century due to the diminishing bison herds on the southern Plains.

could, by attacking Comanche villages in return. In this early struggle, the whites were weak and outnumbered. But during the 1840s and 1850s, the white population of Texas increased dramatically. Behind the settlers, the U.S. government was gathering its own military in support. There was little chance of agreement or compromise, for the Comanche saw themselves as lords of the plains, and they would steadfastly hold to their time-honored customs and their love of fighting.

Chapter 2

Tribal Life: Tradition and Adaptation

When they reached the plains, all the Comanche bands went through an important transformation. No longer gatherers who lived by collecting roots and other plants, they became hunters who supported themselves by killing game. Thanks to the horse, which the Comanche adopted soon after their journey down from the northern mountains, the bands could move swiftly and cover a much greater range. Their ability on horseback transformed them from poor, hungry mountain dwellers into the masters of a vast domain on the southern Great Plains.

Adopting the Horse

Horses were first introduced to the Comanche by the Ute tribe somewhere in the southern Rocky Mountains. By raiding and trading in the settlements of New Mexico, then a colonial province of Spain, the Ute and Comanche were able to build up large herds. From the southern plains, these Comanche horses gradually spread to the east and north until the majority of

Plains Indians were moving, hunting, and fighting on horseback.

The Comanche developed an agility and skill with horses that astonished those who witnessed it. The change took place on a social and even physical level, as artist George Catlin explained in his book *North American Indians*:

> In their movements [the Comanche] are heavy and ungraceful; and on their feet one of the most unattractive and slovenly looking races of Indians I have ever seen; but the moment they mount their horses, they seem at once metamorphosed, and surprise the spectator with the ease and grace of their movements.[9]

This affinity for horses enabled the Comanche to complete the transformation that had begun with their migration away from their Shoshonean homeland. The horse allowed them to roam over a much larger range, since previously they had only dogs as beasts of burden. Horses also allowed the Comanche to hunt more efficiently. Mounted on horseback, they could outrun and surround their prey, if necessary. They could transport more freshly killed meat to their homes. They could also travel longer distances to trade their goods.

The Comanche Hunt

When they reached the plains, the Comanche bands found that game was abundant, much more abundant than in the mountains, where antelope, deer, and other species were much scarcer. Most important, the Comanche encountered vast herds of North American bison rumbling across the plains. The bison moved north during the summer and south again, toward the Comancheria, in the fall as the weather turned cold. The herds supplied many essentials for the Comanche and for the other Plains Indians, including meat for food and hides for clothing and shelter. Each year the Comanche took part in a communal bison hunt in the late spring and early summer. This was the best time of year to collect hides, for the animals were fat and slow-footed after several weeks of feasting on spring grass. (Another hunt took place during the winter,

Each year, in late spring and early summer, the Comanche went on communal bison hunts.

25

Betting on the Ponies

Horses provided the Comanche with important entertainment in the form of racing and gambling. When in camp, Comanche riders tested their horses over short race courses. They also pitted riders against each other in contests of horsemanship. In *The Comanches: Lords of the Southern Plains*, historians Ernest Wallace and E. Adamson Hoebel recount a contest between white soldiers and a group of Comanche at Fort Chadburne, Texas:

"After the first bets had been laid, the Comanches innocently brought forth a miserable-looking pony with a three-inch coat of thick hair and a general appearance of neglect and suffering. Its rider 'looked big enough to carry the poor beast on his shoulders' and was armed with a club with which he belabored the animal from starting line to the finish. Yet, to the surprise of the whites the Indian pony managed to win by a neck. Within an hour the officers bit again and lost by a nose. Then they suggested a third race and brought out a magnificent Kentucky racing mare. In a frenzy of excitement the Indians bet everything that the whites would take. With the starting signal the Indian rider threw away his club, gave a whoop, and his little mount 'went away like the wind.' That Kentucky mare was soon so far behind that for the last fifty yards the Comanche sat backwards on his pony beckoning to the white rider to come on. The whites afterward learned that the shaggy pony was a celebrated racer, and that the Comanches had just come back from fleecing the Kickapoos to the tune of six hundred ponies with that same little horse."

when bison hides were thicker and thus made warmer clothing, blankets, and robes.)

The Comanche hunted either individually or in hunting parties. During a group hunt, the entire village left for the hunting grounds, and a hunt leader was appointed or agreed on to lead the hunt. Once the village reached the hunting grounds, the men prepared their horses and weapons while the women built a temporary camp, raising shelters for sleeping and racks for drying meat.

One of the most common forms of group hunting was the "surround." After finding the herd, the hunters left camp early in the day. They approached upwind of the bison, then formed a circle around the herd. After a signal from the leader, the hunters ran their horses around the circle, gradually forcing their quarry into a smaller area. The hunters then chased down individual animals, pursuing them from the back and using a bow or lance to hit the vital organs behind the animal's rib cage. A few hunters were posted outside to chase down any stray bison that might escape the surround.

The End of the Hunt

Comanche hunters worked together, but according to the rules of the hunt, the dead bison belonged to the hunter who had killed it. He proceeded to butcher the animal, removing the meat and organs and placing them in sacks made out of the skinned hides. While the hunters were butchering the animal they had killed, a lookout—sometimes a man, sometimes a horse—was posted to watch for scavengers or human enemies. From time to time, the hunters looked up from their work to glance at their horses, for they had learned that the big, timid animals would wiggle their ears if they sensed danger.

At the hunting camp, the fresh meat was loaded onto a travois, a simple cart without wheels that was towed by a

Simple carts called travois were used to tow fresh meat back to camp.

horse or dog, and transported back to the main camp. Comanche women then took over the work of slicing the meat into thin strips and hanging them out to dry. The bison hides were scraped of their flesh and sinew and then stretched out between pegs on the ground to dry. They were fashioned into robes, blankets, and the outer coverings of tepees. The paunch of the bison could be turned into a container for carrying water, and its excrement could be used as fuel for campfires. Bison bones and horns made sturdy utensils, including spoons and cups. Its thick hair could be twisted into rope and its sinews made into excellent bowstrings.

The Roles of Men and Women

In the Comancheria, men took the lead in matters of hunting and war. But many Comanche women also took part. They learned to ride with the same skill and daring as the men and were just as eager to display their courage in battle. In 1836, a white captive named James Hobbs accompanied a raiding party south into Mexico. According to Stanley Noyes,

> The great raiding party, [Hobbs] reported, penetrated as far south as Monclova. Surrounding that town of about two thousand residents, the marauders killed forty or fifty mexi-

Glorious Deeds

Winning honors in battle was one sure way to advance to the position of chief among the Comanches. In 1832, the historian Jean Louis Berlandier gave the following description of the career of a successful warrior, as recounted by Thomas Kavanagh in *Comanche Political History.*

"When a warrior wins great honor by mastering his enemy with the knife in face-to-face combat, he covers himself with glory, there is talk of his achievement in council, and as his deeds increase in daring, he gains a degree of respect from his fellows and visibly takes on authority. Then finally, in one of these public assemblies where the pipe passes from hand to hand as the men deliberate, he is addressed as 'captain,' and he acquires the rights to that position. An old man from the council, or the village crier, tells the whole village of his glorious deeds, and as a sign of respect to the mighty warrior, the other men of the village, as well as the women, refrain from smoking before him. Slowly, and almost imperceptibly, he gains power and prestige and is finally named chief."

canos, taking twenty scalps. There was nothing unusual in this, of course. But Hobbs went casually to describe the individual who rode before this army—a young Comanche girl, looked on by the warriors as a kind of "angel of good or ill luck." Riding a fast horse, the girl preceded the line of battle, leading charges, as expert a horsewoman as she was an archer. Evidently the war chiefs of the party later believed their success in this campaign to be owing, in part, to the girl's boldness and cool daring.[10]

When the Comanche were living in the Rocky Mountains, the women and men of the tribe had shared most of the responsibility for gathering and providing food. But when the tribe moved down onto the plains, and hunting largely replaced gathering, for the most part women lost their role as providers. Hunting, a male activity, became a principal source of prestige. On the plains, women carried out the demanding but menial tasks of cooking, skinning meat, setting up camp, and transporting household goods. They had few rights and were considered the private property of their fathers and, after marriage, of their husbands. Yet they did have the right to divorce—as long as they were

Women who were taken captive by Comanche bands were often held as prisoners and servants.

taken in by another husband, who was obligated to reimburse the first husband for his lost property. In cases of divorce, the woman was obligated to leave her children behind.

The Comanche often took women as captives. Most were held as prisoners and servants and were beaten and otherwise mistreated. Sometimes the women were made wives, in which case they had the protection of their husbands. As the village wandered far and wide, return home became increasingly difficult, sometimes impossible. Even when the captives had the chance to return to their former homes, they sometimes refused. Historian Stanley Noyes reports,

> Dr. John Sibley, surgeon and acting Indian agent for the U.S. Army post at Natchitoches in 1805, had reported the occurrence to Washington. Some twenty years previously, it appeared, the Comanches had kidnapped the daughter of Chihuahua's governor general. This distraught official somehow managed to send a thousand dollars to a comanchero to obtain her release. After a short time, the trader succeeded, no doubt paying the captors in goods. But to everyone's amazement, the girl chose to remain with the People. She sent her father a message saying she was married, possibly pregnant, and that her captors had tattooed her. She would be more miserable if she returned, she said, than if she remained with the tribe.[11]

This young woman's experience illustrates the emphasis the Comanche put on expanding their bands by any means possible.

Courtship and Marriage

The Comanche saw large families and sprawling villages as signs of prosperity and wealth. Many Comanche women died young, however, and others suffered miscarriages or the death of infant children. Thus, although the bands often ransomed their captives or traded them for more useful goods such as weapons or horses, they also took young children for the purpose of increasing their numbers. By the same token, the occasion of a wedding, which brought the promise of children, was an event of great importance.

For a Comanche boy, marriage was saved until he had experienced the man's world of hunting and raiding. A bride-to-be and her family demanded that their prospective family member earn the respect of his fellow warriors—by performing courageous deeds witnessed by others—before being accepted as a husband. The girl's family also expected a generous gift of horses and other property before considering the marriage. A suitor would often give the girl's family presents of property that he had captured on raids to express his interest and to demonstrate his ability and daring. He also might agree to undertake raids or to work for a time for the family of his bride-to-be.

Many Comanche girls married when they were very young—some even before they reached puberty. After the gifts had already been given to the family of the girl, a close friend or relative of the suitor presented a proposal. The girl's male guardians—her father and brothers—would then gather to make the final decision, which they often announced in a way that left no doubt. If they accepted the boy into the family as a new son-in-law, they made a show of bringing his gift-horses into their own herd. If they decided to reject the proposal, they returned the horses and all other presents to the disappointed suitor.

The Comanche women sometimes changed bands through marriage, but this

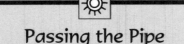

Passing the Pipe

Whenever an important decision was to be made by the chief and elders of a Comanche village, a council was assembled. Before any discussion could take place, however, a ceremonial smoking of a pipe had to occur, as described by the Spanish colonial official Juan Francisco Ruiz in Thomas W. Kavanagh's *Comanche Political History*.

"When a council is to be held it is held in the Chief's tent, and called and managed in the following manner. A fire is built in the center of the Chief's tent, and in the back part of the tent opposite the door is a small enclosure made up of green branches of trees. The Chief takes the principal seat and sends the crier to give notice to all the warriors to come to the council of the pipe. . . . All the men having entered and seated themselves (no woman is allowed to attend), a profound silence reigns in the meeting. . . .

The Chief then fills his pipe from a pouch in which he carries tobacco mixed with leaves of another quality, everyone holding his nose to prevent inhaling the smoke before the ceremony commences. The Chief then lights the pipe and draws a mouthful of smoke, then turns his face towards heaven and blows out the smoke

which ascends to the top of the tent. This is intended as an offering to the sun. He again fills his mouth and turning his face towards the earth blows the smoke downward and then blows smoke first to the right and then to the left. After this he draws from the pipe four times and swallows the smoke, then passes the pipe to the next person. . . . In this way the pipe is passed all around smoked by every one in the same manner as by the Chief, each one after smoking rubbing himself all over. This is continued until three pipes of tobacco are consumed, the chief carefully preserving the ashes.

Consultation then commences. It is determined how long they shall occupy their position, when they shall move their encampment and where they shall re-encamp, etc. If any person arrives during the council from another town or from an expedition, the crier announces it to the Chief, who orders that he be summoned to appear. He then presents himself without speaking to any person in the town until after he has passed through the same ceremonies of smoking. He then tells whence he comes, his adventures, the news he brings, etc., which the crier communicates by shouting through the town."

practice was strongly discouraged by parents of girls. According to tradition, a Comanche bride moved in with the family of her new husband, but the husband was obliged to help, support, and protect her parents as they grew older. Thus if a girl left the band, her parents could not count on the support of her husband. If no young men lived with the older couple, they would eventually have to depend on the charity of other members of the band in order to survive.

"Marriage Groups" and Polygamy

Among some Comanche bands, marriage remained "all in the family." Many Comanche men married a younger sister of the woman their brother had married. Several brothers might marry several sisters. The entire group of husbands, wives, sisters-in-law, and brothers-in-law from two separate families formed a "marriage group" (the Comanche did not allow people who were related to each other by blood to marry). While a husband was away on a hunt or raid without his brothers, one of them took the lonely wife into his immediate family. Comanche women who were widowed often moved into the household of a brother-in-law permanently, as did any children from the marriage.

When they were ranging freely in the Comancheria, the Comanche also practiced polygamy, when one man has two or more wives. Polygamy was common among the more wealthy Comanche leaders, who could afford to support large households. The polygamous man's other wives may have been the younger sisters of his first, or principal, wife, or they may have been women captured on raids and brought into the household as "secondary wives," who were expected to help the principal wife with tasks such as cooking food, skinning game during a hunt, and packing and unpacking household goods during a move from one camp to the next.

The favored wife held authority over the others and sometimes had her own separate tepee in which to live. She also enjoyed a more leisurely life, for the household chores and drudgery were given to those wives with less seniority and status. Favorite wives were known as "sitting beside" wives, because they sat next to their husband in the central tepee, in the place of honor. According to an old Comanche tradition, when a polygamous man died, his favorite wife was also put to death and placed beside him in his grave.

A Comanche Childhood

Comanche parents gave most of their attention and affection to their sons. Girls held a lower position in the family, and this unequal status would never change. A few Comanche girls were chosen as favorites. They were given the finest clothes and possessions and were excused from doing most household chores. They also had the right to select their husbands. Most girls could only express an opinion on a future mate, an opinion that no brother or father was obliged to consider.

Little girls had dolls or miniature tepees to play with, but many also learned how to rope and ride horses and use bows and arrows. When they reached puberty, they began painting their faces in the colors Comanche women favored: red, orange, and yellow, with a vermilion stripe sometimes running along the part of the hair. It was also common to paint the insides of ears, around the eyes, and on the cheeks.

Comanche boys spent much of their time learning how to tame and handle horses. They also practiced skills that

The two wives of Comanche leader Quanah Parker stand in front of their husband's memorial.

they might need in a future battle. They learned how to hang at the side of a horse at a full gallop and fire arrows at the enemy from underneath the horse's neck. Another important skill was retrieving a wounded comrade from the ground, for it was a disgrace to leave anyone behind to be scalped or otherwise mistreated by an enemy. To learn this skill, Comanche boys drilled themselves over and over. They rode two at a time on either side of a person lying prone on the ground, picked the body up, and then rode away.

When they reached puberty, Comanche children took part in a family celebration and feast. Girls would sometimes take part in a simple rite: Hanging on to the tail of a pony, they ran over the plains, hoping to acquire, by magic, the animal's traits of physical strength and agility. A boy's family might celebrate with a bison hunt, in which the boy would perform an admirable or courageous deed that marked his transition to adulthood. These traditions identified the youngster as a full-fledged member of the tribe, one who now shared responsibility with the other adults for the well-being and protection of the village.

The Comanche Villages

Although they belonged to a powerful and far-ranging nation, Comanche families felt their strongest ties to the villages where they lived. The villages themselves did not rest in a single place. Since their migration, the Comanche had

been a nomadic people who moved to several different places in the course of a year. Each new camp was selected with great care, and the scouts who rode ahead to search for the best location took many things into consideration. There must be no way for an enemy to approach the village without being seen (canyons and ridges were favored as good places for protection in case of attack). There also should be a handy source of timber, a source of fresh water, and forage for the horses. A large village could extend for a long distance; in some places it might take several hours to walk from one edge of the camp to the other. According to historians Ernest Wallace and E. Adamson Hoebel, "A large camp sometimes extended several miles along a stream or forest edge. A Comanche village which lay east of the Wichita Mountains in 1834 is reported to have extended along Cache Creek from Medicine Bluff north to Chandler Creek and southward to Wolf Creek, a distance of fifteen miles."[12]

Within the village, a central tepee or lodge housed the chief and his family. Other village leaders had their households nearby. Made of bison hides and supported by stout lodgepoles, the tepees were designed for mobility; they could be put up and taken down in a matter of minutes. A pit was dug in the center of the tepee for the fire, which was kept going all day.

On the edges of the village the Comanche women set out the racks and

Comanche villages consisted of tepees that were made out of bison hides and supported by stout lodgepoles.

scaffolds used for the smelly jobs of drying meat and preparing hides. Preparing food and cooking over the fire was the duty of the women and girls of the household. Bison meat was a staple for the Comanche. They also ate the meat of deer, bear, and antelope, and cattle taken on raids from ranches in Mexico and Texas.

Comanche meals often included fruits such as parsimmon (pictured).

In general, the Comanche ate twice a day, once in the morning and once again, a larger meal, in the evening. Meat was prepared by roasting it over a fire or by stewing it in a pot, if the family happened to have obtained one through trading. Brains, liver, entrails, kidneys, and other organs were often eaten raw. The Comanche also continued to eat fruits such as juniper berries, prickly pear fruit, persimmon, and wild plums. They gathered nuts as well as wild potatoes, wild onions, corn, and pumpkin. For seasoning they sometimes used wild honey. For long-term storage, they prepared pemmican, the traditional Great Plains meal of berries and nuts mixed with dried and pounded meat, to which bison fat was added. The pemmican was stored in animal paunches and could be kept for months, supplying the family when the weather was cold and game grew scarce.

Tribal tradition prohibited them from eating any animals associated with water, such as fish; they also would not eat fowl. When food was scarce, however, the Comanche would butcher one of their own horses or, if necessary to prevent starvation, eat fish, frogs, lizards, rats, squirrels, snakes, and roots.

The changing of the seasons, the coming of the bison hunt, or news of better water, forage, and protection elsewhere might prompt the chief and the elders to move the camp. When the time came, the village set out in a long, single-file line, with men and boys riding out ahead to scout the land and ensure that none of the pack animals strayed too far. By the end of the eighteenth century, the Comanche people were pitching their camps over the vast region known as the Comancheria, and their constant wandering was bringing them into contact with a dozen other large tribes, including the Ute, the Apache, the Kiowa, the Caddo, and the Wichita. They were also meeting European settlers and traders and, at the start of the nineteenth century, people who called themselves Americans.

Chapter 3

Rivals on the Plains

On the Great Plains, where many different Native American nations competed for food and other resources, trade was vital for survival. The Plains Indians did not know iron-making or gunsmithing, so they could not forge their own arms, ammunition, or iron utensils. Only through a constant exchange of goods (and dangerous long-distance raiding) could they obtain the tools and weapons they needed. As historian Walter Hagan relates,

> The Comanches needed these [European] traders. The buffalo provided them everything from the raw material for their lodges to the meat that was the basis of their diet. Nevertheless, the Comanches had come to depend upon other items available only from the Comanchero [trader from New Mexico] or his eastern counterpart. The hard bread, sugar, and coffee these traders brought to the plains enriched the Comanche diet,

and the firearms, kettles, and metal tools simplified the Indian's struggle for existence. The Comanches were nomads, but even the Quahadas had become dependent on trade goods long before they became reservation Indians.[13]

Trade was also the crucial ingredient in the rivalry between the Spanish and French, who arrived in the Comancheria from different directions. The Spanish colonists of New Mexico feared a French invasion of their territory. For a long time, the Spanish saw the Comanche as a protective barrier against the French traders who came from posts on the eastern edge of the plains, where the French had established the colony of Louisiana.

As they collected arms, ammunition, and horses, the Comanche bands increased their range and mastery of the southern plains. By the middle of the eighteenth century, the Comanche were absolute masters of what is now central and western

Texas and neighboring regions. They were raiding as far east as the Sabine River and across the Rio Grande, deep into Mexico. When the Comanche broke with the Ute, Spanish officials formed an alliance with the Ute and with anyone else they believed could help them stop the terrifying Comanche raids against their settlements. At the same time, the Comanche were also embroiled in a long-standing rivalry with the Apache, themselves widely feared warriors and raiders.

The Comanche and Apache

The Apache, like the Comanche, were divided into several independent bands, which included the Mescalero, the Jicarilla, and the Lipan. Their rivalry with the Comanche began when the Comanche migrated into the territory between the San Saba River and the Rio Grande in what is now southern Texas. Within just a few years of their first encounter, the Comanche were constantly fighting with the Apache. In 1725 the two sides battled for a

The Comanche and the Apache, rivals after the Comanche migrated into the territory between the San Saba River and the Rio Grande, battle against buffalo hunters.

week along the Rio de Fierro (Wichita River). The Apache were more skilled in mountainous and broken country, as they fought with stealth. The Comanche fought better on the open plains, using quick, hit-and-run raids staged over long distances. By the middle of the eighteenth century, the Comanche superiority in the plains had turned the tide: They had driven the Apache bands completely out of the open country of the Comancheria.

The Spanish of New Mexico had been using the Apache as a buffer against the Comanche. Now, with the Apache retreat, Spanish outposts such as Pecos Pueblo were raided, their horses were stolen, and many women and children were taken captive by the Comanche. After the French sold the vast Louisiana Territory to Spain in 1762, and both western and eastern borders of the Comancheria came under Spanish control, the Spanish sought a truce. At first, it was refused. The Comanche continued raiding the settlements until 1786, seven years after New Mexico governor Don Juan Bautista de Anza defeated a prominent Comanche chief in battle. According to the terms of a treaty with de Anza, the Comanche were granted safe passage to Santa Fe, the capital of New Mexico. The Spanish governor also promised to hold annual trade fairs that the Comanche could attend peacefully. The end of the treaty session was described by historian Stanley Noyes:

De Anza, as a token that war had ended, presented Chief Ecueracapa with a saber and a banner. The Co-

manches responded by digging a hole in the earth in which they symbolically buried the war. On the following day, under de Anza's personal supervision, the Spaniards held a trade fair in which the visiting Comanches bartered hides, meat, tallow, a few horses, and three guns. Afterward they expressed their gratification and spoke of transferring most of their trade to Pecos Pueblo.[14]

By the treaty of 1786, the Spanish also undertook the task of building a permanent village, San Carlos, on the Arkansas River for a Comanche band. Although de Anza hoped the Comanche would settle down and peacefully begin farming, this part of the treaty would prove a failure. The Comanche had taken up the life of nomads and hunters, and they would never adapt to farming. In a very short time, they abandoned San Carlos.

After the treaty was signed, the Ute joined the Jicarilla Apache to carry on the fight against the Comanche. But the Comanche, armed and on horseback, had attained a strength and a range that no other tribe could match. Their raids against the Apache had driven that tribe permanently from the southern plains, across the Pecos River to the west, and across the Rio Grande to the south. No alliance of Ute, Apache, or any other tribe of the plains or mountains could stop the Comanche, who now held undisputed sway over the Comancheria.

Problems on the Reservation

The reservation shared by the Comanche and other tribes proved by and large a miserable place to live, beset by poverty, corruption, and hopelessness. In her book *Women of Oklahoma*, Linda Williams Reese describes the conditions of the resevation through the eyes of Charles E. Adams, the agent placed in charge of the Comanche and other tribes in Oklahoma.

"Agent Charles E. Adams also found the Indians under his care sadly behind in all of the factors that indicated acculturated behavior. In his report to the Commissioner of Indian Affairs in 1891, Adams included the 1,151 Kiowa with the 1,624 Comanches, 325 Apache, and 1,066 members of various smaller tribes in his jurisdiction. Of the total 4,166, only 12 percent had wholly or partially adopted white dress. Indians occupied 197 of the government-built houses; the rest continued to live in tipis. Less than 10 percent could use enough English for conversation and just a slightly higher number could read. . . .

Reservation administration during this period reeked of incompetence, corruption, fraud, and failure. Cattlemen, peddlers, miners, gamblers, and whiskey merchants invaded the reservation, duping the less-knowledgeable Indians. An-nuity payments and rations arrived unpredictably and, often, late. Unscrupulous traders bartered spoiled and inferior goods for high prices. Politically influenced appointments, nepotism, and low salaries plagued the institutions that were responsible for acculturation by providing employment for individuals who were unfit or unsuited for work."

This newspaper illustration depicts the corruption of the reservation administration.

Friendship with the Kiowa and Cheyenne

The Kiowa, like the Comanche, moved down into the plains from the northern Rocky Mountains, where they had been living near the headwaters of the Missouri River in what is now central Montana. They first took up a new homeland in the Black Hills but were driven from that region by the Sioux in the eighteenth century. Their first meeting with the Comanche at the Arkansas River quickly led to warfare, which lasted until 1790, when the northern bands of the Comanche arranged a truce with the Kiowa. Sixteen years later, the Comanche and Kiowa agreed to end their warfare and arrange a permanent peace.

According to Kiowa tradition, this occurred when Comanche and Kiowa parties came separately to the house of a comanchero trader and interpreter, Juan Lucero, in New Mexico. Before a fight could break out, the comanchero arranged a council between the two hostile peoples. A Comanche named Afraid of Water invited a Kiowa, Wolf Lying Down, to spend the summer in his camp. Wolf Lying Down agreed to visit the Comanche camp and discuss a permanent truce. He told the Kiowa with him that if he had not returned by the time the leaves turned yellow, his friends should consider him dead and avenge his murder.

Wolf Lying Down went to the Comanche camp, married a daughter of Afraid of Water, and returned before the fall to assure his followers that the two peoples were now friends and that a permanent truce had been arranged.

A generation later, the Kiowa and the Comanche also made peace with the Cheyenne and the Arapaho. Just before this agreement, the northern bands of the Comanche had been fighting with the Cheyenne in the vicinity of the Arkansas River. At the same time, a small outpost known as Bent's Fort was trading actively with the Cheyenne and bringing other tribes into contact, and occasional rivalry, with each other. But in the winter of 1839, after the marriage of an Arapaho and a Kiowa Apache, the four groups decided to meet the next summer at Bent's Fort. A great meeting was held along the Arkansas in the summer of 1840.

To show their new friendship, the Indians exchanged presents, each side trying to outdo the other in generosity. By this time, the Comanche and Kiowa had collected the largest horse herds on the Great Plains. Every Cheyenne received several horses as presents, and one Kiowa chief gave away 250 head. In return, the Cheyenne hosted an enormous meal of food acquired peacefully from Bent's Fort and made a gift of valuable trade goods that the Comanche lacked, such as kettles, blankets, guns, and ammunition. From that point on, the four tribes were at peace.

The Comanche and the Five Civilized Tribes

In 1830, the Choctaw, Creek, Cherokee, Chickasaw, and Seminole began arriving in the lands west of the Mississippi River. These tribes were referred to by the people of the United States as the "Five Civilized Tribes," because unlike the Plains Indians, many among them had settled down to farm, had raised permanent villages, and had adapted to the ways of the whites. Nevertheless, many in the United States did not believe that Native Americans could be successfully brought into their nation. Thus Congress passed the Indian Removal Act of 1830, which forced the Five Civilized Tribes to move to a strange and hostile land far from their homes. They had to fend for themselves at a time when game was diminishing and white settlement was just beginning to reach the eastern fringe of the Great Plains. The Comanche as well as the Kiowa and other tribes already living on the southern plains considered the eastern tribes to be intruders on their hunting grounds. Because these new tribes came from the east, the direction from which American settlers were also arriving, the Comanche also suspected them of being allies of the whites.

The Comanche began raiding the resettled tribes, attacking their settlements, and

A Chief of the Kotsoteka

As the Comanche began encountering the United States and its people, certain Comanche leaders emerged as spokesmen and representatives of the tribe. Although the Comanche saw themselves, more or less, as a community of equals, the Americans wanted to deal with certain individuals who held leading positions, just as generals, presidents, and business executives did in their own society. One of these Comanche leaders was Mowway of the Kotsoteka. According to historian James L. Haley in *The Buffalo War*,

"The Kotsotekas . . . boasted only one influential chief, though he was indeed a dominant personality: Mow-way (Push Aside). His acclaim for bravery was truly widespread; in the scalplock over his craggy face was strung a gigantic claw, a trophy taken from a grizzly bear that the chief killed with a knife as the animal was mauling one of his braves. . . . He always represented himself to the Americans as friendly, having boasted on receiving a government medallion that he had never made war on Washington; during the 'Winter Campaign' of 1868 the military agent listed him as a valuable friend of the government. His good will, however, did not extend to Texans and Mexicans, and he was jailed for raiding in Santa Fe, New Mexico, in 1869. He also was outspoken in his displeasure with Indians who settled on the reservations as long as there were buffalo to hunt, as he told the Alvord Council [a treaty commission] in 1872 that, to bring him in to the reservation, 'I was promised lots of things, but I don't see them. . . . When the Indians in here are better treated than we are outside, it will be time enough to come in.'"

The westward expansion of the United States posed a threat to the Comanche's way of living.

burning their homes. In 1853, the Comanche joined with four other tribes to fight the eastern nations. The campaign ended in a great battle along the Kansas River, where the Comanche and their allies were defeated by a group of better-armed Sauk, Fox, and Potawatomie Indians. After this defeat, the Comanche held to their territory in the Comancheria and ceased raiding to the north and east.

Contact with the Five Civilized Tribes, and with the early American settlers on the plains, did not persuade the Comanche to change their ways. They were raiders, warriors, and hunters, and they would resist any attempt to convert them into settled farmers, even into the twentieth century. The drastic differences between their lives and those of the whites, and the gradual westward expansion of the United States into their territory, made a violent clash almost inevitable.

A Clash of Cultures

In the 1820s, the earliest American settlers in Texas crossed the Sabine River to claim land in what was then Spanish territory. For a time, the Comanche and the Americans lived in peace. The whites had not yet ventured as far west as the Comancheria, and they seemed to represent no threat to the Comanche bands that roamed there. In 1835, however, the American settlers revolted against the authority of Mexico, and in 1836 they established the independent Republic of Texas. This event marked the beginning of a long-standing war between two very different cultures, both fighting for the same land, unable to peacefully coexist with each other.

Refusing to recognize the Native American claims to the land, the game, or the

The Indian Problem

In *The Comanche People*, Joseph H. Cash and Gerald Wolff describe the effect that the Indian Removal Act had on the troubled frontier that lay between the Comancheria and the new territories of the United States.

"In establishing the policy [of removal], they [the U.S. government] completely forgot that the areas into which these people were to be removed were already inhabited. As a result, the eastern tribes met with considerable hostility and were scarcely welcomed by their brethren in the west. The eastern Indians brought with them better weapons than the Plains Indians possessed and a knowledge of the techniques of the white men. They killed off many of the buffalo, and there were minor clashes between the new and old tribes in the area. In 1854 [1853 according to some sources], a major struggle developed when approximately fifteen hundred Kiowas, Kiowa Apaches, Cheyenne, Arapahoes, Osage, and Comanches combined in an attempt to exterminate the intruders near the Smokey Hill River in Kansas. There they met a party of Sauk, Fox, and Potawatomie Indians who were very well equipped and who killed approximately twenty of the attackers and wounded many others during the ensuing battle. Apparently only six of the intruded Indians were slain. Thus, the Comanches and their allies had met defeat at the hands of other Indians, but Indians who were as foreign to them as the white man."

hunting grounds, the Texans moved steadily southward from the Red River and westward from the Sabine. There were no legal agreements, or agreements of any kind, made between the Texans and the Indians. The settlers simply drove wagons and horses into the river valleys and the vast plains of Texas, bringing their farming tools, their household goods, and their weapons.

The Texans claimed plots of land near rivers and creeksides, where fresh water and grass were more plentiful. They built houses of wood or sod, often using the barbed branches of the osage orange plant to raise fences around their claims. The makeshift barricades served both to corral livestock and to keep out strangers.

By building permanent homes, the settlers showed that they had no intention of moving according to the season, as the Comanche and other nomadic Native American tribes did. And by establishing fenced domains, they demonstrated their belief that they owned the land and everything on it—the grass, trees, rocks, and water. Strangers who might cross it, hunt on it, or try to use it in any other way were regarded as enemies. To deal with their enemies, the Texans built walled fortifications. From these secure areas, they roamed the plains to seek out and destroy Indian villages and hideouts.

Although the whites were well armed, the Comanche were not deterred from their customary raiding. The small and isolated white settlements made inviting targets. Indeed, the superior quality of American horses, which were of English stock and thus larger and stronger than the Spanish horses, attracted constant raiding by Comanche braves.

The first Texas president, David Burnet, attempted to forge a treaty with the northern bands of Comanche in 1837, but the Comanche refused to cede any of their lands. At a meeting in San Antonio in 1838, the Comanche asked for a permanent frontier between themselves and the Texans and also for trading posts where they could buy and sell goods. Their proposals were rejected, and soon afterward the Texas government established a series of frontier posts intended to protect the settlements. Gradually, this line of forts would be extended westward.

Land Rush and Forced Relocation Increase Problems

The trouble between the Comanche and the Texans grew more serious in the 1850s after Texas achieved statehood. A new wave of homesteaders arrived in search of what they regarded as "free" land in central Texas. This land rush pushed several Native American tribes, including the Waco, Tonkawa, and Wichita, westward and deeper into the Comancheria, while the eastern, "removed" tribes of Cherokee and others began raiding from their homes in eastern Oklahoma. In their struggle to survive in the traditional way, these tribes began

Battle Honors

The Comanche and neighboring tribes all had different ways of dressing, talking, building their homes and villages, and fighting. Their battle methods varied even down to the practice of counting coups, as Stanley Noyes explains in *Los Comanches*.

"After leading a series of successful raids, the warrior would, over a few years, acquire a reputation for his valor, good sense, and the potency of his medicine; which, in a superficial way, might be equated with 'luck.' Because he was a Plains Indian, he would also have gained prestige by such war honors as stealing horses from an enemy camp, taking scalps, and counting coups. The coup (French for 'blow,' which can also carry a suggestion of 'deed') was a far greater honor than collecting a scalp.

Specifically it signified the touching of an enemy with the hand or, among the Cheyennes, a specially striped 'coup-stick.' The Comanches, though, might apply the word to other daring deeds. The People [Comanches] gave credit for a blow by two separate warriors on the same individual. The Cheyennes allowed three touches, each by a different man, while the Arapahoes permitted four. Touching a dead foe during battle gained one the honor, but the greatest deed was to touch a living enemy, an act that could be extremely dangerous, even if the man were fallen and dying."

hunting bison and other game the Comanche considered their own. As overpopulation threatened, the resources of the land diminished. The Comanche found the bison and other game fast disappearing and their own hunting range gradually reduced.

In the meantime, the encounter with the whites was creating deeper divisions of the old Comanche society. The southern Comanche bands, including the Penetheka, the first to encounter the Americans, learned to trade with them peacefully. Others, particularly the Yamparika and the Quahadi, remained hostile. The Comanche nation began its split into traditionalists, who would refuse to adapt, and progressives, who would sign treaties and soon put an end to their raiding.

Reservations: An Unacceptable Suggestion

Many whites all over the United States believed that the Texans could not farm, ranch, or raise their families in safety unless the Comanche were eliminated from the southern plains altogether. To stop the conflict and to ease the way for permanent white settlement, the United States proposed a system of reservations. Large plots of land—preferably land that white farmers did not want—would be reserved for each tribe of Indians. With the help of government food rations and the guidance of white teachers, missionaries, and agents, the Native Americans could settle down on the reservations and begin an entirely new life as peaceful farmers.

Most of the Comanche met the reservation plan with fierce resistance. They made it known that they would not live on a reservation, no matter how large. They saw farming as a low-status occupation, fit only for people who could not hunt or fight. The Comanche had never been farmers. They were nomads who moved with the seasons and with the migrating herds of bison.

The Loss of the Bison: A Disastrous Development

No matter how skilled and daring on horseback, or how accurate with an arrow or a

A man sits on top of a mound of bison hides. Bison—the Comanche's main source of food, clothing, and shelter—were being slaughtered without restraint by white settlers.

lance, the Comanche could not stop the slaughter of their principal source of food, clothing, and shelter. The bison herds provided an easy target for white hunters who were seeking hides, especially those of mature females, which they could sell in the trading posts along the rivers of the Great Plains. The Indians limited their hunts to certain seasons, usually the late spring and early summer, but the whites killed millions of bison—as many as they could take—regardless of the season. Beginning in the mid–ninteenth century, the great herds that had once covered the plains like a vast black cloud began to shrink.

In the space of about thirty years, from 1850 until the mid-1880s, the North American bison practically vanished from

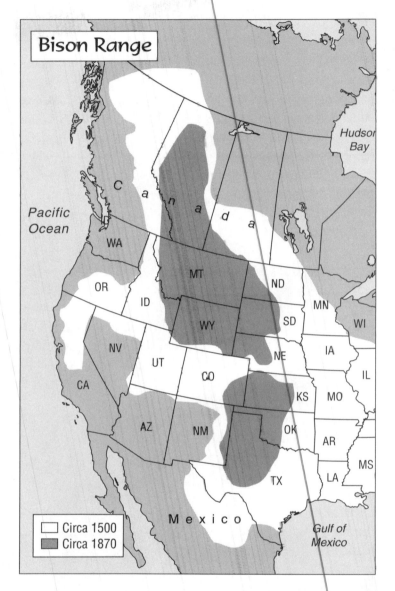

the Great Plains. By the 1880s, only a few thousand bison were left and the species was nearing extinction. The loss of the bison herds was one of many reasons for the wave of Comanche raids on the ranches and settlements of Texas in the 1850s and early 1860s. These raids were the best way the Comanche knew of to fight for their survival. Since their migration from the northern mountains, they had been a nation of warriors, and now they were in the most difficult fight they had ever known: a fight for their survival as an independent people.

Chapter 4

War and Conflict

Among the tribes that knew them, the Comanche enjoyed a reputation as the fiercest warriors on the Great Plains. There was nothing boastful or exaggerated about such claims, and for a Comanche man, there was no more worthy occupation than making war on an enemy. It was as a warrior that the Comanche earned the respect of his family and the other members of his band. All Comanche measured themselves and others by a single standard: their ability to fight and their willingness to die in battle.

The Comanche distinguished between three different kinds of fighting: raids, war campaigns, and vengance attacks. Raids were undertaken to secure horses as well as the captives needed to bring new members to the band and the village. During war campaigns, a large group was assembled for the purpose of killing as many of the enemy as possible and claiming new hunting grounds. Vengeance attacks were undertaken to settle serious grievances, such as the murder or capture of a clan member. No Comanche could rest until the death of a companion or relative,

A Comanche earned the respect of his family and peers by exhibiting courage in battle.

particularly a brother, was re-
venged by the death of the enemy
responsible.

War Chiefs

At some point, a young Comanche warrior prepared his
own war party, an act that all
considered the mark of having
reached full-fledged adulthood. Before the group was assembled, the warrior sought a
vision or dream to gather the
inspiration of the spirit world
for his campaign. He would
then invite other men in the
village to join him for a council, during which he would describe the vision and the fight
he wished to lead. At the council the warrior would pass a
ceremonial pipe. The pipe
symbolized friendship, agreement, and a promise. Those
who wanted to join the fight,
and who felt sufficient respect for the
leader's ability, would smoke. Those who
did not wish to join the expedition would
refuse the pipe and pass it along to the
next man. That evening, the warriors gathered to take part in a war dance and to
hear the good wishes of those who would
stay behind.

The Comanche took the matter of good
fortune seriously. They believed that supernatural powers guided their successful military leaders. The *puha*, or sacred power, was
a vital part of the makeup of the Comanche

*Comanche "war chiefs" presided over councils
when it was time to make important decisions.*

warrior. The best leaders, those who enjoyed
the help and blessings of the guardian spirits,
became "war chiefs" who led Comanche
councils when it was time to make an important decision about raiding or warfare.

The War Party

The war parties of the Comanche set out
late at night or early in the morning, a time
when the new light of the eastern sky was
thought to bring good luck. The group

51

The Comanche and the Colt

Warfare on the wide-open southern plains demanded good horses as well as the best weapons available. Both sides had to adapt—the Comanche by learning to use muskets and rifles obtained through trade and the whites by modifying their own weapons to shoot as straight, as far, and as fast as possible. According to Ian Frazier in *Great Plains*,

"The Comanche had a lot to do, indirectly, with the development of the handgun. The first time the Texas Rangers used Samuel Colt's new revolving pistol in a fight with [the] Comanche was the first time they whipped them. The revolver was the perfect horseback weapon against an enemy who could shoot twenty arrows and ride three hundred yards in a minute. It amazed the Comanche, who remembered that encounter for generations. The Rangers made suggestions to help Colt improve his gun, and gave him his first fame."

The Colt .45 (pictured) evolved from the Colt revolver that was used by the Texas Rangers to fight the Comanche.

might ride many miles over rugged country to reach their target (Comanche raids in Mexico, for example, began on the other side of the Rio Grande, two hundred miles or more to the north). The members of the party prepared themselves by painting their faces, their bodies, and their horses. They brought their best arrows, circular shields made out of bison hides, lances, and, when they had them, rifles.

The Comanche approached their target silently, under the direction of the war chief who had brought them together. When the time was right, they might let out a terrifying yell and begin charging at full gallop. They attacked in the middle of the day, when the enemies might be resting, or at night, the best nights being those with no moon. The warriors split up into small groups and rode through the enemy camp. They captured horses and goods, burned houses, and killed anyone found in the streets or their homes. Women were brutally attacked and sometimes tortured. Women as well as children were taken captive, tied fast to a spare horse or forced to walk the long distance back to the camp of the raiders.

The Comanche fearlessly raided the camps of enemy tribes, trading posts, hunting camps, white towns, farms, ranches—anywhere goods and people were readily available for capture. They attacked from an ambush or, when their numbers were so great that resistance would be useless, they pursued an enemy across an open plain. At all times, they tried to avoid casualties. The loss of a single Comanche warrior could be disastrous to the members of his family and to others in his village who depended on him for food and protection.

The Comanches and the United States

In 1845 Texas was admitted into the United States. With their change in status to U.S. citizens, Texas fully expected the U.S. military to protect them from the Comanche raiding parties. Although the Texans wanted to drive the Comanche from their state entirely, federal policy favored the reservation system. Despite the Comanche tribe's longstanding opposition to the idea of being confined, the United States sent many companies of mounted, blue-coated warriors into the Comancheria to build forts and to fight the Indians with rifles, revolvers, and cannon, all in an effort to persuade the Comanche chiefs to surrender and "come in" to the reservation.

From time to time, when the fighting grew most serious, the U.S. government would send a commissioner into Comanche territory to arrange a truce. This official would invite a group of chiefs to assemble near a fort or trading post and promise to distribute presents. Before the meeting, the Comanche and the whites assembled as much firepower as they could and put on the most warlike appearance possible.

After offering a peace pipe, the Comanche would rise to make their demands and their speeches. They always asked the whites to stay out of their territory, while the whites always asked the Comanche to stop committing their raids. A treaty would then be drawn up by the whites, signed by the commissioners and agents present, and marked by the Comanche, who had no written language.

Often the agreements that were reached resulted from the Comanche's poor understanding of certain provisions. In any event, the Comanche leaders could not prevent their young warriors from seeking the battle honors that were so important to them. And more important, only a portion of the entire Comanche tribe, a single band or two, would appear at each council to put their marks to a treaty.

Nevertheless, in 1855, the Texans agreed to give up a small parcel of their land in order

Comanche Battles

The Comanche always sought the honor that came with a brave act, to be seen and remembered by companions. This could be accomplished during battle. Once the Comanche had joined in a battle, the war leader no longer gave orders; he could only inspire his followers by example. Whenever the Comanche faced a strong enemy out in the open, however, the war party began working together. They formed a great circle around the enemy, gradually riding in closer and closer while shooting their arrows and firing their guns. If the enemy gathered forces and made a charge through the shrinking circle, the Comanche would retreat. They would ride to another part of the battlefield, a hill or canyon where they could regroup their forces for a counterattack.

This tactic was effective against other tribes and against lightly armed homesteaders surprised in the open. It was suicide, however, when the enemy had artillery. The Comanche battle method had another major drawback in that it did not allow for a long siege against an enemy stronghold, such as Adobe Walls. For this reason, the Comanche usually could not defeat fortified ranches or trading posts that were protected by timber walls. Eventually, the Comanche and the other Plains Indians were defeated by the superior resources and greater numbers of the white invaders.

Comanche war tactics were not effective against enemy strongholds such as Adobe Walls.

The number of Comanche raids on the Texas frontier escalated after the Civil War began.

to bring about a truce. This first Comanche reservation lay along the Brazos River in north central Texas. Although few members of the Penetheka band came in to the reservation to settle permanently, the great majority of Comanche remained off the reservation and continued their fighting and raiding against the settlements.

This Comanche reservation would vanish in less than a decade. Threatened by attacks from the whites, the reservation Indians were moved north of the Red River in July 1859. In the Comancheria, soldiers and settlers were destroying Comanche villages and killing many warriors. Then came the great conflict that divided the United States in two.

The Civil War and the Comancheria

The Civil War changed the Comanche's situation for the better. When the federal troops were called on to fight the armies of the Confederacy, which the state of Texas had joined, several forts in the Comancheria were abandoned. In fact, the war left the Texas frontier and its settlements largely unguarded against the Comanche raiding parties.

General warfare erupted on the Texas frontier in the summer of 1863. During this time, the Kiowa and Comanche stepped up their raiding on the whites as well as on their traditional enemies, the

Settlers Celebrate a Victory

The clash between Texas settlers and the Comanche brought some of the bloodiest fighting anywhere on the Great Plains. Accidental meetings ended in fights to the death; the trophies of battle were weapons and human scalps. On June 28, 1860, a party of Texans set out to avenge a Comanche ambush in which a white woman had been scalped. In "A Chapter in the History of Young Territory," Texas historian Fannie McAlpine Clarke reports on the return of a party that had killed thirteen Comanche Indians on Paint Creek:

"The occasion was celebrated by a public barbecue on the square in Weath-erford, at which stirring speeches were listened to by a vast assemblage from every portion of the surrounding country. In the evening a dance was given at the court house, and on a rope stretched diagonally across the large room were hung the arms and equipments captured by the party and also the scalp of the white woman, as well as those of the slain warriors—gruesome decorations for a scene of festivity. General Baker exhibited these trophies of the Paint Creek fight in many other places, and everywhere among the settlers arose the cry, 'Exterminate the Indians.'"

Caddo of southern and eastern Texas. The Comanche raided all over the southern plains at will. They attacked horse herds as well as cattle herds, selling the cattle to a U.S. Army in need of provisions. They also attacked wagon trains using the Santa Fe Trail, which ran along the Arkansas River.

The Confederate army set up its own posts in Texas, while in Kansas and along the Arkansas the federal government placed Union commanders in charge. Treaties were signed but never respected, and planned punitive expeditions against the Comanche were not carried out. All available troops were di-verted away from their posts to fight Confederate raiders on the frontier to the north.

As the Civil War drew to a close, the Confederate army dreamed up a plan to have the Comanche and the Kiowa fight on the side of the South. But this plan was never carried out. At the end of the war in 1865, the fighting and raiding grew worse. While the federal and state governments were at odds over which would take responsibility for protecting the western frontier, the Comanche began driving settlers away, back to the east. Content with their victory, the Comanche did not even bother to come in for treaty goods that had been promised to them.

The Medicine Lodge Treaty

The problems in Texas prompted the U.S. Congress to authorize another treaty commission in 1867. This time, the council was held at Medicine Lodge Creek in Kansas. During the council, a Comanche chief named Ten Bears made a powerful appeal for understanding from the white commissioners. His words on behalf of his people had no effect, however. According to the Medicine Lodge Treaty that was signed on October 21, the Comanche would allow the whites to build railroads and roads and military posts in the Comancheria. In return, the government would supply seeds, tools, and lessons in farming, as well as an annual payment of money and goods, for the next thirty years. In addition, a reservation was set up for the Comanche, Kiowa, and Kiowa Apache to share. The boundaries were the 98th meridian on the east, the Washita River on the north, and the

During the council held at Medicine Lodge Creek (pictured), Comanche chief Ten Bears delivered a powerful speech on behalf of his people.

Red River on the south. Altogether the reservation covered 3 million acres.

The Comanche were one of the last tribes of North America to give up fighting against the United States. They were most reluctant to give up the fight against the people of Texas, who by the time of the Civil War represented their most feared and hated enemy. In 1871, four years after the Medicine Lodge Treaty that was supposed to bring a permanent peace to the southern plains, several bands of Comanche were still carrying out raids. In one great gathering, a group of Kiowa, Comanche, and Kiowa Apache attacked the Butterfield stagecoach trail. The raiders captured a wagon train and brutally killed five people. This massacre inspired a campaign of revenge by the whites under the leadership of General Philip Sheridan. This campaign would eventually bring about the total surrender of the last Comanche holdouts.

Ten Bears Speaks

At Medicine Lodge Creek in 1867, the Comanche leader Ten Bears made the following Comanche declaration of independence to a group of white treaty makers, as quoted in Wallace and Hoebel's *The Comanches*:

"You said that you wanted to put us upon a reservation, to build us houses and make us medicine lodges. I do not want them. I was born upon the prairie, where the wind blew free and there was nothing to break the light of the sun. I was born where there were no enclosures and everything drew a free breath. I want to die there and not within walls. . . . When I was in Washington the Great Father [President Grant] told me that all the Comanche land was ours, and that no one should hinder us in living upon it. So, why do you ask us to leave the rivers, and the sun, and the wind, and live in houses? Do not ask us to give up the buffalo for the sheep. . . .

If the Texans had kept out of my country, there might have been peace. But that which you now say we must live in, is too small. The Texans have taken away the places where the grass grew the thickest and the timber was the best. Had we kept that, we might have done the things you ask. But it is too late. The whites have the country which we loved, and we only wish to wander on the prairie until we die. Any good thing you say to me shall not be forgotten. I shall carry it as near to my heart as my children, and it shall be as often on my tongue as the name of the Great Spirit. I want no blood upon my land to stain the grass. I want it all clear and pure, and I wish it so that all who go through among my people may find peace when they come in and leave it when they go out."

Quanah Parker and the Battle of Adobe Walls

It was during this time that Quanah Parker rose to become war chief of the Quahadi band. Quanah was the son of a chief named Nokoni and Cynthia Ann Parker, a white woman who had been captured as a child during a raid on her parents' Texas home. Under Quanah's leadership, the Quahadi attacked settlements and cattle ranches all over central Texas and in the Panhandle of northern Texas. They ambushed hunting parties, coach stations, and any stray whites found wandering on the southern plains.

But Quanah Parker had been unable to prevent the great land rush that occurred after the Civil War, when thousands of new settlers moved ever farther west across the plains. The Quahadi found themselves surrounded like a herd of bison during the spring hunt. They were forced into a smaller and smaller area, while the bison—their main source of food, clothing, and shelter—all but disappeared, slaughtered by well-armed parties of white hunters. Even in

Quahadi war chief Quanah Parker (right) led attacks on settlements and cattle ranches all over central Texas and in the Panhandle of northern Texas.

the rugged Staked Plain, the Quahadi had fewer and fewer places in which to hide.

In the spring of 1874, Quanah Parker and a prophet named Ishatai joined forces to lead a final campaign against their enemies. Ishatai had inflamed the people by his preaching and had led a four-day religious observance, a sun dance. Thus prepared, the Comanche, accompanied by several hundred Cheyenne and Kiowa warriors, set out on the morning of June 27. The warriors gathered on the hillsides surrounding the isolated hunting outpost of Adobe Walls, which lay near the south fork of the Canadian River.

There were twenty-five men and one woman inside the three small buildings at Adobe Walls. Although the attack began early in the morning, the settlers had been up half the night repairing a cracked roof beam and thus were not surprised in their sleep. The whites collected ammunition, food, and water, quickly barricaded their doors and windows, and armed themselves with powerful, long-range bison guns.

While Ishatai watched from a hilltop, the Comanche rode in waves down on the settlement and killed two men who were outside sleeping in a wagon. The Comanche attacked with great yells and whoops, but their arrows and rifles could not breach the strong walls or barricaded doors of the buildings. The defenders poured a deadly fire into the enemy, and the Comanche saw their companions fall, unprotected by the strong medicine (power) Ishatai had claimed to possess.

One Comanche fighter named Cohayyah witnessed the battle:

We lost the fight. The buffalo hunters were too much for us. They stood behind adobe walls. They had telescopes on their guns. Sometimes we would be standing way off, resting and hardly thinking of the fight, and they would kill our horses. One of our men was knocked off his horse by a spent bullet fired at a range of about a mile. It stunned, but did not kill him.[15]

The defeat at Adobe Walls signaled the end of the fight against the white settlers from the east. The result of the clash was inevitable. A growing, populous, and industrializing nation had swept aside a small hunter/gatherer society whose main source of food had vanished. The Comanche would now have to adapt to a new life, or disappear completely.

The Surrender of Quanah Parker

In the summer of 1874, the cavalry posted to Indian Territory undertook one last campaign to end the Comanche threat to the frontier. In September, three months after the battle of Adobe Walls, Colonel Randal Mackenzie of the Fourth Cavalry attacked a large Comanche encampment at the head of Palo Duro Canyon in northern Texas. The battle was over quickly, with the Comanche the losers.

In May 1875, Colonel Mackenzie sent an interpreter and messenger, Dr. J.

Joe Horner's Statement

Texans who had trouble with the Comanche fought back with all the means at their disposal, including lawsuits. In a sworn statement given in court while trying to recover damages from the U.S. government, which his family held responsible for the losses it had suffered at the hands of the Indians, Joe Horner, a Texas cattleman, filed this statement, as given in Robert De Arment's *Alias Frank Canton*:

"I hereby certify in the year of 1873 I owned cattle in Jack, Young, and Palo Pinto Counties in Tex. and was riding the range every day. At that time the Comanche and Kiowa Indians was raiding upon our frontier, their depredations were so frequent that on nearly every 'light of the moon' some frontiersman would lose his scalp and have his horses stolen and driven off by those Comanche and Kiowa Indians to the Fort Sill Reservation where they seemed to be safe from arrest or pursuit. The only way we could keep our horses in those days, at night on the light of the moon, was to either put them in a corral and stand guard over them all night, or to wait until daylight was gone. Then quietly drive them off to the mesquite flats, hobble them all out to graze, and sleep on our saddle blankets until daylight."

J. Sturms, from the army post at Fort Sill into Quanah Parker's camp along the White River in western Texas to make an offer: If the Quahadi would come into the post peacefully, they could live in the vicinity of Fort Sill without harassment by the army or by civilians. If not, they would all be hunted down and killed like wolves. Seeking the guidance of the Great Spirit, Quanah Parker left for a vision quest into the wilderness. There he witnessed the signs that pointed him and his people in the direction of Fort Sill and a final surrender. According to W. S. Nye,

From this time on, Quanah, who was possessed of superior intelligence, shrewdness, and force, seemed to increase his influence over the Comanches. It was not long before he had completely overshadowed the older chiefs, and was recognized by the whites as principal chief of the Comanches. This was something they had never had before. On June 2, Quanah, accompanied by most of the Quahadas, arrived at Fort Sill. There were 100 warriors, 300 noncombatants, and 1,400 ponies. The men were disarmed and their ponies were sold at auction.[16]

The battle for Texas and for the Comancheria had ended. The Comanche would have to give up their nomadic life and, somehow, live as the whites did. The surrender marked the end of fighting on the southern plains, but there would be more battles to fight, battles in which the Comanche would struggle to hold on to their language, their culture, and, perhaps most important, that part of their lives that expressed their highest aspirations and their most deeply held beliefs: their traditional religion.

Chapter 5

Religion

In the past, some historians called the Comanche people the "atheists of the Plains." Compared with the practices of other Plains tribes, and indeed with the piety of many American pioneers and settlers, the Comanche did not seem to make religion an important part of their lives. They had no powerful class of medicine men or women, and they had few group ceremonies. Instead, each individual developed and followed a personal spiritual path, seeking the help of guardian spirits in times of danger or need or when important decisions had to be made.

Ishatai and the Sun Dance

Ishatai was one of the few individuals renowned among the Comanche for his

Shoshone men participate in a sun dance. Unlike other tribes, the Comanche had few group ceremonies.

spiritual power. A member of the Quahadi band, he claimed the power to spit bullets out of his stomach, predict the future, and speak directly with the dead. In the spring of 1874, finding his people desperate, Ishatai persuaded all the Comanche bands to gather together for a sun dance.

Ishatai did not invent the sun dance, which was a test of endurance and a source of spiritual renewal practiced by the Kiowa and by other Native American tribes living on the Great Plains. But he knew of it and had seen the warriors of other tribes subject themselves to the exhausting ceremony, in which they danced for many hours, stared directly into the sun, and tore their own flesh. Ishatai believed that if the Comanche could finally unite themselves through a great sun dance, the Great Spirit would return their fearlessness and fighting ability and help them to defeat the whites once and for all.

The defeat at Adobe Walls quickly brought the Comanche down from the spiritual peaks they had attained during the sun dance. On the way home from the battle, they denounced Ishatai's fraudulent claims to having supernatural powers.

Ishatai believed that the sun dance (pictured), a test of endurance and a source of spiritual renewal, would unite the Comanche with the great spirit and make them fearless warriors.

Some may have criticized themselves, as well, for having yielded to the temptation to follow such a man.

Traditional Beliefs and the Vision Quest

Among the Comanche, no medicine man or community initiation was needed to assist a person seeking *puha*, which always arrived with a vision or dream. For the Shoshone peoples of the mountains, magical visions might come unexpectedly in the middle of the day or night. But for most of the Plains Indians, a vision had to be sought out, a belief that brought about the practice of the "vision quest." For a young Comanche, the first vision quest was an important sign that he was now taking part in the life of adults, which entailed all the responsibilities and opportunities possessed by the elders. (The vision quest could be taken only by a male. A Comanche woman acquired her sacred power through the help of her husband, and even then she could not use the power until after her husband had died or she had reached the age of menopause.) The vision quest was a solo journey. The seeker would leave his family and village behind to spend four days in a place

A First Dream

To a medicine doctor, or to any Comanche, sacred power always made itself known in the form of dreams or visions. There was an important difference between ordinary dreams and magical dreams; magical dreams might show the dreamer his or her abilities or help make an important decision. In *Sanapia: Comanche Medicine Woman*, author David Jones quotes Sanapia's description of her first magical dream.

"This man, something like a man, came to where I was sleeping way in the night. He stood there and then held his hand to me. I just watch him, you know. I wasn't scared or nothing. Then he move his arm toward north and all at once I saw his arm go away from him. And next morning I said, 'You all know what, I'm sure lonesome to see my uncle. He's up north around Geary. Let's go see him, if you all want to.' Here we pack up and beat it down there north. And we was coming. We visit him about four days or five days. I said, 'Uncle, we going, home now.' He said, 'Why?' and I told him, 'Just feel I get home and get my cheek.' Then he went back and opened up his suitcase and said, 'Come here,' and I went. He had about twelve eagle feathers and he told me to take one I want best. I pulled out the best one in the bunch, and he said, 'That's for you. Take it with you.' And so that feather, what I dream about was given to me by my uncle. That's what that dream, really good dream, carried with it."

The Peyote Ceremony

In her book *Oklahoma: Foot-Loose and Fancy-Free*, written in the 1940s, author Angie Debo describes the peyote ceremony followed by the Comanche and other Native American tribes in the state that had once been "Indian Territory."

"Some Indians find in 'Father Peyote' a more indigenous religion than the white man's expression of Christianity. This small 'button' of cactus was used ritually by the tribes of Old Mexico at least four centuries ago. The cult reached the Comanches and Kiowas about 1880, and spread tribe by tribe through the western half of the Indian Territory. The government tried to stamp it out, and so in 1918 the Indians—advised, it is said, by a distinguished ethnologist—incorporated the Native American Church under Oklahoma law in order to claim the protection of the statutes for religious freedom.

The worshipers meet in a ceremonial lodge for an all-night session of prayers, exhortations, and ceremonial eating of the peyote—all in an atmosphere of peace and fraternity, with liberal borrowings from Christian and native ideology. The drug can bring nausea, anxiety, terrifying hallucinations, and a frightening disintegration of personality 'as if I could throw my arms out and my arms left me, went off in the air, and I felt I was going all to pieces.' But in this religious atmosphere it brings flowing sensations of color, beatific visions, and a mystical sense of union with the Infinite. It never incites to violence, it is not habit forming, and it seems to have few, if any, damaging aftereffects."

A Comanche leader of a peyote cult.

of sacred power such as a hilltop or at the gravesite of a respected ancestor.

To prepare himself, the seeker sought the help and advice of an elder member of the tribe, one renowned for his religious knowledge and ability. Before setting out, he took a ritual bath to purify himself. He also collected sacred articles, including a pipe, tobacco, and a flint to produce a fire. The seeker then left his home and village, and four times on the journey he stopped to smoke the pipe and pray to the unseen spirits whose power he was seeking. As the first night fell, he prepared himself. According to historians Wallace and Hoebel,

> As darkness approached, he smoked and prayed for power, for good power, and that he might use it for good. He covered himself with the buffalo robe at night as he lay facing the east, and he had to keep his head covered the whole night through. Rising at daybreak, he faced the east to receive the benefit of the power radiating from the sun.[17]

The seeker waited for the vision to come. It might appear as an eagle or coyote that crossed his path or as a sudden storm that erupted from a cloudless sky. The vision made the young Comanche aware of his particular ability and power. It revealed the sacred songs and objects that would assist him in "making medicine" in the future. It also revealed anything that was forbidden to him or dangerous. From that point on, the young Comanche's guardian spirit would stay with him for the rest of his life. The spirit might be associated with certain animals or certain places, which would unleash the *puha* that the seeker had discovered on his first vision quest.

As an adult, the Comanche continued to seek guidance from the spirit world through vision quests. For example, when Quanah Parker had to decide whether to accept reservation life on behalf of his people or to defy the government agents and soldiers, he rode away from the camp and climbed a large mesa. There, with a bison robe drawn over his head, he prepared to make this choice, the most important of his life. Historian Bill Neeley describes Quanah's struggle:

> He would rather die than surrender. But should he lead his people to their death? He despised the reservation Indians who planted crops and drew subsistence from the agency, but he thought of his mother. Perhaps he could learn the white man's way. Down on the flat ground below the mesa, a rangy wolf turned his head toward Quanah and howled, then trotted off to the northeast, toward Fort Sill. Above him an eagle glided lazily and then whipped his wings in the direction of Fort Sill. These were signs from the Great Spirit.[18]

Sacred Things

After the vision quest, the Comanche brought the powers of the spirit world down into their daily lives. In the morning, a Comanche might sing to prepare a day of good fortune. After a successful chase for bison in the spring, hunters would thank the spirits with a chant. To cure a sickness, a medicine doctor prayed to the unseen world for a healing vision.

Everyday objects could be imbued with supernatural power by ceremony or incan-

In order to heal their patients, Comanche medicine men prayed to the unseen world for a healing vision.

tations. These objects made up a Comanche's "medicine bag." The medicine bag contained sacred things associated with the vision quest and with the guardian spirit. The claws of animals or the talons of birds could inspire courage or impart skill in tracking, finding, and killing game. Eagle feathers might protect and assist the wearer in a coming raid or expected battle; stones might bring a long life and physical endurance.

Carried at the side or around the neck, the medicine bag brought good luck and power when necessary. Men carried medicine bags while on a hunt or engaged in warfare. Children were given them by parents to ensure their survival and good health. Women about to give birth gathered their sacred articles about them, seeking the protection of friendly spirits. Certain herbs were also used by men and women for protection or for the healing of sickness or injury.

Although the Comanche respected an individual's practice of magic and use of amulets and sacred objects, Comanche society did have strong traditions against the harmful uses of magic. The use of power also carried taboos—forbidden places, objects, or actions that if violated would bring bad luck. The possession of supernatural power carried with it a great responsibility, and the Comanche did not risk incurring a spirit's anger by trying to use the power without faith or with bad intentions. Indeed, the Comanche sometimes rethought their decision to acquire *puha*. Traveling back to the place where they had obtained their guardian spirit's medicine, they would ceremonially return the amulet or other sacred object to the wild.

Medicine Men and Women

Certain individuals within Comanche society were recognized as *puhakat*, or medicine men and women. They were people who had knowledge in the ways of magical protection, healing, and guidance, and whom other band members credited with powerful magical abilities. They were shamans and healers who were believed capable of directly communicating with the Great Spirit and with the unseen spirit worlds. At one time, these *puhakat* played a vital role in the life of the Comanche. They also served as tribal leaders, making important decisions and resolving disputes. But when the Comanche moved down onto the plains and the bands grew more warlike, *puhakat* declined in importance and were replaced by war chiefs.

Individuals who were recognized as *puhakat* still took the responsibility of healing other members of the group. When in need of a cure or good luck, the Comanche would approach a *puhakat*, through either a family member or a friend. In this way, the medicine men—and women—continued in their old role as healers.

Some medicine practitioners had special tepees set aside for the practice of their art. Before they could practice, Comanche doctors went through several years of training. They learned the rituals associated with gathering certain plants used in healing. They learned how to prepare and use the plants, how to diagnose illnesses, and how to treat patients. They learned how to bring their own power—their *puha*—against the bad spirits or medicine that caused the trouble.

Comanche doctors also learned the rules of proper conduct. They had to carry themselves in a certain way, and act with their patients and other members in a certain way, at all times. There were right ways and wrong ways to carry on the practice of traditional medicine. According to the training of the Comanche medicine woman Sanapia, as described by David Jones,

An eagle doctor must also be always accessible. He cannot refuse anyone his services. . . . An eagle doctor must never extol his own abilities and should also dissuade others from doing so. . . . A doctor should never suggest that he could cure an individual but must wait for the individual to approach him. . . . A doctor must be paid for his services, no matter how slight. Similarly, a doctor cannot

The Christian Vanguard

The Comache's settlement on the reservation soon attracted missionaries who wanted to live among them. Not all these missionaries confined their mission to instructing Native Americans in Christian teachings. The Reverend E. C. Deyo, who began a Baptist mission on the western edge of the Comanche reservation in 1893, also saw himself leading the vanguard of white settlement. As William T. Hagan observed in *United States–Comanche Relations*,

"Comanches also gave a cool reception to the Reverend E. C. Deyo's efforts to establish a Baptist mission among them. He came to the agency in the winter of 1893–94 and started construction of a church at three or four locations before he found one acceptable to the Indians. Moreover, they did not flock to it once established. In the first four years of its operation the mission gained only eight members although services might attract others on an irregular basis. . . .

Writing the first spring he was on the reservation, Deyo enthused about 'the blessing of having some of our own race with us' and extended an invitation to other whites to worship at the mission. In the columns of a newspaper devoted to hastening the day Congress would open the reservation to whites, Deyo not only referred to his labors 'to prepare the Comanche to meet his God, and dwell with him in heaven forever,' the reverend also anticipated the time when 'these broad prairies may be settled by industrious Christian whites, who will help to roll onward the Grand Old Gospel car.'"

work his Medicine without payment. . . . In addition, the payment, with the exception of certain relatively inexpensive ritual items (green cloth and tobacco) required at the first interview of doctor and patient, must be left to the discretion of the patient. A doctor cannot refuse anything which is offered in payment.[19]

Sanapia, one of the last recognized "eagle doctors" among the Comanche, continued to practice her medicine until her death in 1989. By that time, many of the ancient beliefs and traditions of Comanche religion had been forgotten or been transformed into legends and memories. Only certain forms of traditional ceremony have survived, and few Comanche boys embark on vision quests. For better or worse, the Comanche have changed their ways to suit the modern world, while still honoring ancestors who lived a very different life on the Comancheria.

Chapter 6

The Comanche in the Modern World

The defeat at Adobe Walls in 1874 and the surrender of Quanah Parker in the next year marked the end of the traditional life of the Comanche. The different bands began to settle down for good on the reservation they now shared with the Kiowa and the Kiowa Apache. Many families moved away from their villages and took up a more solitary life. Some turned to ranching, others to raising crops in the dusty, dry soil.

To survive, most of the Comanche depended on regular rations handed out by the government agents. Once a week, the agents gave each Comanche family a certain amount of beef, flour, coffee, and other necessities. At first, the rations were given out through the chiefs, who had the responsibility of ensuring that each family received what was due. Later, the agents gave out the rations to individual families. By doing this, the government deliberately weakened the chiefs' authority over the Comanche people. This effort gained strength when the agency organized a Comanche police force on October 1, 1878. The members of the force had the authority to arrest anyone—even older members who, by tradition, were their superiors—and they enforced rules against fighting, drunkenness, polygamy, dancing, spirit healing, and stealing.

In 1886 the reservation convened its first Court of Indian Offenses. On the court sat three Indian judges—a Kiowa, a Wichita, and, as chief judge, the Comanche Quanah Parker. The court convened twice a month and ruled on minor offenses such as theft, disturbing the peace, holding a prohibited sun dance, or the practice of polygamy. (A U.S. federal court decided serious criminal cases such as murder.) The Indian court also heard civil disputes such as competing claims to land, livestock, or other resources. In some cases, a fine was assessed; in others, rations were withheld for a certain period of time. In criminal cases, a person found guilty sometimes served a jail sentence, which may have been more severe than the sentence he would have faced in a U.S. court.

On July 1, 1901, after functioning for fifteen years, the Court of Indian Offenses was disbanded. On this day, as a result of a treaty known as the Jerome Agreement, the state courts of Oklahoma were given jurisdiction over the Comanche living on the reservation, and whites were allowed to buy land that had been promised to the Comanche. The Jerome Agreement brought a rush of new settlement that would further encroach on Comanche homes and land.

The Jerome Agreement and Its Consequences

In the 1890s, white settlers were still pressing westward, hungry for land on which to establish their own farms and ranches. Many of them looked to the Indian reservations of the Great Plains and demanded that

Native Americans line up for rations. After the defeat at Adobe Walls and the surrender of Quanah Parker, Comanche bands settled down on reservations and began to depend on government rations.

Booker T. Washington Visits Oklahoma

The African American educator and reformer Booker T. Washington was the president of Tuskegee Institute and the most prominent spokesman for African Americans in the early years of the twentieth century. He traveled widely in the United States to bear witness to the living and working conditions of blacks, and during one of these journeys in 1905, he arrived in what was then Indian Territory. In the following letter, reprinted in David Colbert's *Eyewitness to the American West*, a collection of letters, diaries, and newspaper accounts of life on the western frontier, Washington describes the visit.

"In the fall of 1905 I spent a week in the Territories of Oklahoma and Indian Territory. During the course of my visit I had an opportunity for the first time to see the three races—the negro, the Indian, and the white man—living side by side, each in sufficient numbers to make their influence felt in the communities of which they were a part, and in the Territory as a whole. . . .

One cannot escape the impression, in traveling through Indian Territory, that the Indians, who own practically all the lands, and until recently had the local government largely in their own hands, are to a very large extent regarded by the white settlers, who are rapidly filling up the country, as almost a negligible quantity. To such an extent is this true that the Constitution of Oklahoma, as I understand it, takes no account of the Indians in drawing its distinction among the races. For the Constitution there exist only the negro and the white man. The reason seems to be that the Indians have either receded— 'gone back,' as the saying in that region is—on the advance of the white race, or they have intermarried with and become absorbed with it. Indeed, so rapidly has this intermarriage of the two races gone on, and so great has been the demand for Indian wives, that in some of the Nations, I was informed, the price of marriage licenses has gone as high as $1,000."

Booker T. Washington observed that Native Americans were ignored as a race by whites.

the government open them to white settlement. Those in favor of this new policy claimed that, because many of the Indians did not "use" the land and did not consider that they "owned" it, the land should be made available to those who would take title to it and put it to good use.

This argument led to a new government policy known as "allotment in severalty." According to the Jerome Agreement of 1892, each Comanche—every man, woman, and child—would be allotted, or granted, a 160-acre parcel of land. Although the Comanche had the right to use the land as they wished, the allotments would be held in trust by the government for twenty-

Facing pressure from white settlers who desired to move westward, the U.S. government began to sell Indian land.

five years. This was to prevent white speculators from pressuring Indian families into accepting token cash payments for land they would then have to leave. Four large parcels of land totaling 550,000 acres were supposed to be held aside as public lands for the entire Comanche community. After the government made the allotments, the rest of the reservation would be open for settlement by outsiders. For agreeing to give up their lands in this way, the Comanche tribe would be paid a total of $2 million.

The proposed arrangement faced very strong opposition from Comanche leaders who were against selling any part of the reservation, whether it was being "used" or not. Nevertheless, in 1901 the Jerome Agreement was signed into law by the president, touching off an instant land boom in southern Oklahoma. New towns such as Anadarko and Lawton appeared where once there had been wide-open prairie. Drawings were held to determine which settlers would be granted the free, 160-acre homesteads. In 1906, by another law, the four public tracts were also sold off. The last of the reservation lands held in common by the Comanche people disappeared.

Once the most powerful tribe on the southern Great Plains, numbering more than twenty thousand, the Comanches had declined to a group of about two thousand people who no longer even had a government reservation to consider home. Even if they were allowed, somehow, to go back to their traditional ways of nomadic hunting, they would not be able to survive, for the bison and most other wild game had disappeared from the plains. For the Comanche, the land of the Comancheria had been spoiled by the white ranchers and cattle herders. Quanah Parker summed it up: "We love the white man but we fear your success. This was a pretty country you took away from us, but you see how dry it is now. It is only good for red ants, coyotes, and cattlemen."[20]

Adapting to a New Life

Despite all these changes, the Comanche people were slow to accept the new ways. According to James Mooney, writing in 1890,

The Comanche were nomad buffalo hunters, constantly on the move, cultivating nothing from the ground, and living in skin tipis. Excepting that they are now confined to a reservation and forced to depend on government rations, they are but little changed from their original condition. They are still for the most part living in tipis of canvas, and are dressed in buckskin.[21]

Many Comanche felt most strongly about the loss of their community life and the failure of their old religion and medicine to protect them. Some held fast to their traditional language as a last remnant of their free life in the open, unfenced plains. The medicine doctor Sanapia was the daughter of a Christian father and a traditional mother, a situation that often brought conflict to the house. She recalls,

Lots of times I would be playing or something and I have to go with her . . . speak for her. I tell her, "You can talk English good, why do I have to talk for you?" She just tell me to come on. She said that when the white mans learn Comanche talk, she would learn white man language. She was real stubborn, I guess you would say, about things like that. You know, one time my father put these little napkin rings like they used at school on our table and he told us kids to use them. Well, my mother got them and put bead work on them with our name on each one. My father got mad at that, but my mother told him that she wasn't no white man, she was Indian.[22]

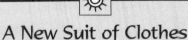

A New Suit of Clothes

Because they could no longer hunt, the Comanche could no longer supply themselves with the bison hides that they used to make their moccasins and clothing. According to the Medicine Lodge Treaty, the U.S. government was supposed to supply the Indians with material for new clothes. But, according to Wallace and Hoebel in *The Comanches*,

"Only a person with a distorted sense of humor could have regarded the selection of articles issued as less than tragic. The black, shoddy suits given out to the men were practically worthless, but some government contractor had been enriched. The trousers were all the same size, made to fit a man of two hundred or more pounds. The shirts were red flannel, and the hats were of a high, puritanical pattern. The Comanches, unaccustomed to the white man's clothes, quickly discarded the hats, although today hardly one can be seen without a hat. The coats were converted into vests by cutting off the sleeves, which the children wore for leggings. The seat was cut from the trousers and the feet from hose to convert both into leggings. Some wore the hose without shoes, and women wrapped the cloth around themselves without the trouble of subjecting it to either scissors or needle and thread."

Native Americans were unaccustomed to the clothing provided by the U.S. government.

Peyote and the Native American Church

As their land and resources were being taken from them, the Comanche adopted a new ritual. At the center of the ritual was the drug called peyote.

Peyote is a desert plant whose roots, or buttons, induce strange dreams and hallucinations in those who eat them. It has been used by Native peoples in Central and North America for centuries. After learning about peyote from the Apache and Indian tribes of northern Mexico, the Comanche turned to the drug as a replacement for the visions that they had once sought by voyaging into the wilderness. Since there was no wilderness left, they began gathering in specially built peyote lodges to access the spirit world through the use of the drug.

At the same time, Christian missionaries were arriving on the Comanche reservation to teach in the schools and to work at the reservation agency (headquarters). Many of these missionaries strongly opposed the use of peyote, but the Comanche resisted any attempt to ban the drug from their reservation.

The debate over peyote continued into the early 1900s. Finally the state of Oklahoma passed a law that recognized the new Native American Church, in which Christian beliefs were practiced in conjunction with the use of peyote. The new law, which legalized the use of peyote in religious ceremonies, remains in effect, but the use of peyote has been challenged in the late twentieth century, as modern American society and the Comanche continue to make difficult adjustments to each other.

The Twentieth Century

The Comanche were not well prepared for the twentieth century. Few Comanche boys or girls attended school past the elementary grades. Most Comanche families suffered poor health and lived in poverty. The struggle grew harder during the Oklahoma Dust Bowl of the 1930s, when even white farmers, desperately seeking the means to support their families, left the state to search for work elsewhere. Without the money or the transportation to leave, many Comanche families remained behind, but some of them did manage to reach southern California, where the Comanche still make up a significant Native American community.

After the Dust Bowl, some members of the Comanche tribe provided important service to the nation that had conquered them. Many Comanche enlisted in the armed forces during World War I. During World War II, seventeen young Comanche took part in the "Code Talkers" program in Europe. The Code Talkers, most of whom were Navajo, used their traditional Native American languages as the basis of a code for secret military communications. Germany, the enemy of the United States in Europe, was never able to break the code. Because of the service rendered by the Comanche during the D day invasion of Europe, the government of France, an ally of the United States, awarded the Code Talkers with a prestigious military medal in 1989.

World War II also brought important changes to the Comanche people who remained at home. According to historian Stanley Noyes,

With the war, many Comanche men left home to serve in the armed forces. Others left the region for defense jobs, since by now most younger Comanches spoke English. Before the war few jobs had been available. People had mostly sat around talking or playing cards or dominoes. But during the

Comanches who lacked money or transportation to move west were devastated by the Oklahoma Dust Bowl.

Stopping the Vote

In 1902, during a congressional election, Quanah Parker found himself drawn into the petty rivalries and endless scheming of American politics. As the leading representative of the Comanche, he was approached by Frank Canton, a local sheriff and Democrat, to thwart a plan to turn his people into Republican voters. The threats made to manipulate the chief are described by Robert De Arment in his book *Alias Frank Canton.*

"Canton and Sheriff Painter remained good friends despite their opposing political affiliation. But friendship did not prevent Canton from blocking Painter's machinations when the November elections neared. A heated fight between Democrat William Cross and Republican Bird S. McGuire for the Oklahoma congressional delegate seat developed that fall. Of course Painter supported McGuire and, as Canton told it in later years, took illegal steps to ensure his election.

'I found out that Captain Painter was planning to vote 500 Comanche Indians at the last minute and so set about to try to put one over on him,' recalled Canton. Knowing that his pal Burk Burnett, a staunch Democrat, and Quanah Parker, the famous Comanche chief, had a long-standing friendship, Canton wrote Burnett explaining the situation and asking for [Burnett to write] a letter to Parker 'telling him not to let his Indians vote.' . . . Burnett warned Parker in his letter that if the Comanches voted, 'they would certainly get in bad with the government at Washington, for they had no legal right to vote [at that time].' Canton added: 'He further told Parker that if they did vote the government would take all of his wives away from him but one, would make his people pay taxes and work the roads. Parker listened to the letter and then he rose and wrapped his blanket about him. He said in a stately manner, "Captain Painter, he good friend, he want Comanche vote republican. Indian agent, he good friend, he want Comanche vote republican. But Burk Burnett he best friend. He say you his friend. Then you Quanah's friend. Comanches no vote tomorrow from this reservation."' Canton said that on election day he 'saw Quanah Parker driving over the country herding in all stray Indians and not an Indian vote was cast that day.'"

postwar years approximately one out of two Comanches left to find work elsewhere. In a physical sense the tribe had dispersed to a marked degree, a condition that persists today, with members returning periodically for family visits or to attend powwows, such as the annual Comanche Nation Fair.[23]

Ironically, the Comanche language itself was beginning to die out. By the beginning of World War II, only a few hundred elderly members of the tribe could speak the language fluently. To survive in the modern world, it was necessary to speak English, and at the missionary schools, Comanche children were given English names and discouraged from using the language of their ancestors.

The Comanche Today

In 1963, the Comanche officially withdrew from the Medicine Lodge Treaty of 1867. The Comanche wrote their own constitution in 1967. Two years later, they signed a formal peace treaty with the leaders of the Ute tribe, an act that ended centuries of warfare and disagreement. To improve the situation of poverty and high unemployment on the reservation, the Comanche Business Council was formed. The council replaced the traditional

Activist LaDonna Harris has worked to reduce the hardships experienced by the modern Comanche.

leadership of Comanche chiefs; the Comanche recognized that in business matters it was more productive to bring together several of their leaders in a cooperative manner to make important decisions.

By the 1990s, the Comanche population had reached about ten thousand. Comanche families have scattered across the southwestern United States, from Oklahoma to California. Members of the tribe have started their own businesses in Lawton and other towns in southern Oklahoma. The Comanche have also followed the example of many other North American tribes by opening a casino, Comanche Nation Games, just south of Lawton.

Along with economic development comes the task of preserving a traditional language while living in a modern and rapidly changing society. This task has been taken up by the Comanche who formed the Comanche Language and Cultural Preservation Committee (CLCPC). The committee helped the tribe adopt an official alphabet and spelling system in 1994. It has published a Comanche dictionary, flash cards, and a monthly Comanche language magazine. The group also leads tours of sites important in Comanche history. In June 1999, the CLCPC marked the 125th anniversary of the battle of Adobe Walls with a visit and commemoration at the battle site.

The Comanche language and identity have, somehow, survived after the disappearance of the Comancheria and the many years of bare survival on a poor reservation in the late nineteenth and early twentieth centuries. However, many

The American Indian Religious Freedom Act

After many years of bitter debate over the use of peyote and the practices of the Native American Church, the U.S. Congress finally took an important step in resolving the matter with the following law, passed on August 11, 1978:

"Resolved by the Senate and House of Representatives of the United States of America in Congress assembled. That henceforth it shall be the policy of the United States to protect and preserve for American Indians their inherent right of freedom to believe, express, and exercise the traditional religions of the American Indian, Eskimo, Aleut, and Native Hawaiians, including but not limited to access to sites, use and possession of sacred objects, and the freedom to worship through ceremonials and traditional rites."

problems remain. Poverty and poor health affect many Comanche families, and many Comanche youngsters are leaving the reservation to find work and live closer to mainstream American society. Some members of the tribe have found themselves embroiled in legal disputes over land titles, over their gambling businesses, and over the use of peyote in religious ceremonies. But with the determination that once marked their hard-fought survival on the open plains of the Comancheria, the Comanche are fighting again to preserve their language, their history, and their identity as a significant and respected Native American people.

Notes

Introduction: The Comanche and the Southern Plains

1. Ernest Wallace and E. Adamson Hoebel, *The Comanches: Lords of the Southern Plains*. Norman: University of Oklahoma Press, 1952, p. 55.

2. Rupert N. Richardson, *The Comanche Barrier to South Plains Settlement*. Glendale, CA: Arthur H. Clark, 1933, p. 19.

3. William T. Hagan, *United States–Comanche Relations: The Reservation Years*. New Haven, CT, and London: Yale University Press, 1976, pp. 8–9.

4. Quoted in Wallace and Hoebel, *The Comanches*, pp. 9–10.

Chapter 1: First Encounters

5. Meriwether Lewis and William Clark, *A History of the Expedition of Captains Lewis and Clark*, Chicago: 1903, p. 36.

6. David E. Jones, *Sanapia: Comanche Medicine Woman*. New York: Holt, Rinehart & Winston, 1972, p. 13.

7. James Mooney, *The Ghost-Dance Religion and the Sioux Outbreak of 1890*. Lincoln: University of Nebraska Press, 1991, p. 1,044.

8. Jones, *Sanapia*, p. 11.

Chapter 2: Tribal Life: Tradition and Adaptation

9. George Catlin, *North American Indians*. New York: Viking, 1989, pp. 74–75.

10. Stanley Noyes, *Los Comanches: The Horse People, 1751–1845*. Albuquerque: University of New Mexico Press, 1993, p. 98.

11. Noyes, *Los Comanches*, p. 91.

12. Wallace and Hoebel, *The Comanches*, p. 15.

Chapter 3: Rivals on the Plains

13. Hagan, *United States–Comanche Relations*, p. 13.

14. Noyes, *Los Comanches*, p. 81.

Chapter 4: War and Conflict

15. Quoted in W. S. Nye, *Carbine and Lance: The Story of Old Fort Sill*. Norman: University of Oklahoma Press, 1969, p. 191.

16. Nye, *Carbine and Lance*, p. 235.

Chapter 5: Religion

17. Wallace and Hoebel, *The Comanches*, p. 157.

18. Bill Neeley, *The Last Comanche Chief: The Life and Times of Quanah Parker*.

New York: John Wiley & Sons, 1995, pp. 143–44.

19. Jones, *Sanapia*, p.28–29

Chapter 6: The Comanche in the Modern World

20. Quoted in Harold J. Langer, *American Indian Quotations*. Westport, CT: Greenwood Press, 1996, p. 87.

21. Mooney, *The Ghost-Dance Religion and the Sioux Outbreak of 1890*, pp. 1,045–1,046.

22. Quoted in Jones, *Sanapia*, p. 21.

23. Stanley Noyes and Daniel J. Gelo, *Comanches in the New West, 1895–1908*. Austin: University of Texas Press, 1999, p. 28.

For Further Reading

Dee Brown, *Hear That Lonesome Whistle Blow.* New York: Simon & Schuster, 1977. The story of the railroads, including their effect on the Native Americans of the Great Plains and their role in bringing white settlement to the West.

Joseph H. Cash, and Gerald W. Wolff, *The Comanche People.* Phoenix, AZ: Indian Tribal Series, 1974. A short anecdotal book on Comanche origins, history, dress, religion, and modern reservation life.

William T. Hagan, *Quanah Parker, Comanche Chief.* Norman: University of Oklahoma Press, 1993. A short and well-researched biography of Chief Quanah Parker.

David E. Jones, *Sanapia: Comanche Medicine Woman.* New York: Holt, Rinehart & Winston, 1972. A study of the life and ways of the last surviving traditional medicine practitioner, or "eagle doctor," written by her adopted son.

Bill Neeley, *The Last Comanche Chief: The Life and Times of Quanah Parker.* New York: John Wiley & Sons, 1995. A biography of Quanah Parker that describes how the Comanche leader was transformed from a skilled fighter into a charismatic and respected civil leader among the Comanche during their difficult transition to reservation life.

Willard H. Rollings, *The Comanche.* New York: Chelsea House, 1989. Part of the Indians of North America series, this is a richly illustrated overview of Comanche history and traditions, with detailed accounts of daily life on the Comancheria.

Ernest Wallace and E. Adamson Hoebel, *The Comanches: Lords of the Southern Plains.* Norman: University of Oklahoma Press, 1952. A standard scholarly work on the Comanche that provides vital details backed by years of study and first-person accounts of traditional Comanche life and history.

Works Consulted

George Catlin, *North American Indians*. New York: Viking, 1989. Written during an expedition lasting from 1832 to 1839, this is a comprehensive description of Native American tribes and their leaders by a skilled portrait painter from Pennsylvania, who was escorted into the frontier territories by explorer William Clark.

David Colbert, *Eyewitness to the American West: From the Aztec Empire to the Digital Frontier in the Words of Those Who Saw It Happen*. New York: Viking Press, 1998. A collection of first-hand accounts—letters, newspaper and journal articles, diaries, memoirs, and essays—dealing with early exploration, settlement, development, and current events and issues in what is now the western United States.

Mary B. Davis, ed., *Native America in the Twentieth Century*. New York: Garland, 1994. An encyclopedic collection of more than three hundred articles about contemporary Native Americans.

Robert K. De Arment, *Alias Frank Canton*. Norman: University of Oklahoma Press, 1996. The colorful story of Joe Horner, alias Frank Canton, a desperado, frontiersman, and lawman. This controversial figure roamed Texas and the southern plains as well as Wyoming and Alaska and provided a prototype for the western novels of Rex Beach and Owen Wister.

Angie Debo, *Oklahoma: Foot-Loose and Fancy-Free*. Norman: University of Oklahoma Press, 1949. A history of white settlement and development in the state that began as the Indian Territory.

T. R. R. Fehrenbach, *The Comanches: The Destruction of a People*. New York: Da Capo Press, 1994. Authoritative and comprehensive history of the Comanche and their defeat in the 1870s.

Ian Frazier, *Great Plains*. New York: Farrar, Straus, and Giroux, 1989. An anecdotal exploration and informal history of the plains states.

William T. Hagan, *United States–Comanche Relations: The Reservation Years*. New Haven, CT, and London: Yale University Press, 1976. A study of the Comanche from the Medicine Lodge Treaty until the Jerome Agreement and the opening of the Comanche reservation.

James L. Haley, *The Buffalo War*. New York: Doubleday, 1976. An account of the massacre of the bison, the principal natural resource of the Plains Indians, in the middle and late nineteenth century.

Stanley Hoig, *Beyond the Frontier: Exploring the Indian Country*. Norman: University of Oklahoma Press, 1998. A description of the major explorations through the southern Great Plains and of life as it was lived by Native Americans in that region before white settlement.

Thomas W. Kavanagh, *Comanche Political History: An Ethnohistorical Perspective, 1706–1875*. Lincoln: University of Nebraska Press. A very long and very thorough study of archive sources—describing the relations both within the Comanche tribe and with white traders and settlers—that began with an investigation into a political dispute among the modern Comanche.

Harold J. Langer, *American Indian Quotations*. Westport, CT: Greenwood Press, 1996. A well-illustrated, informative, and useful collection of historical and contemporary quotations from representatives of Native American peoples, commenting on their encounters with white civilization and the problems they confront in contemporary America.

David Lavender, *Bent's Fort*. Garden City, NY: Doubleday, 1954. An exciting chronicle of adventures and encounters along the Santa Fe Trail and within the trading post known as Bent's Fort in southeastern Colorado.

Meriwether Lewis and William Clark, *A History of the Expedition of Captains Lewis and Clark*. Chicago: A. C. McClurg & Co., 1903. The diaries of the leaders of the Missouri River expedition of 1804–1806, the first explorers to cross North America from the Great Plains to the Pacific Ocean.

James Mooney, *The Ghost-Dance Religion and the Sioux Outbreak of 1890*. Lincoln: University of Nebraska Press, 1991. An account by ethnologist James Mooney of the Ghost Dance troubles among the Sioux, which ended in the Wounded Knee Massacre, and an encyclopedic account describing the customs, homes, and languages of dozens of Plains and mountain tribes in the early 1890s.

Stanley Noyes, *Los Comanches: The Horse People, 1751–1845.* Albuquerque: University of New Mexico Press, 1993. A study of the Comanche, disguised as a novelistic narrative, that tracks events until 1845.

Stanley Noyes and Daniel J. Gelo, *Comanches in the New West, 1895–1908.* Austin: University of Texas Press, 1999. A slim volume of historical background and full-page reproductions of photographs taken on the Comanche reservation in the late 1890s and early 1900s.

W. S. Nye, *Carbine and Lance: The Story of Old Fort Sill.* Norman: University of Oklahoma Press, 1969. An account of cavalry companies and their battles around Fort Sill written by a lieutenant of artillery who researched the book during the 1930s.

Linda Williams Reese, *Women of Oklahoma, 1890–1920.* Norman: University of Oklahoma Press, 1997. An account of settlement and early statehood seen through the eyes of Oklahoma's women pioneers.

Rupert N. Richardson, *The Comanche Barrier to South Plains Settlement.* Glendale, CA: Arthur H. Clark, 1933. A scholarly account of Comanche-white relations and encounters throughout the nineteenth century.

Index

Idaho, 10
Indian Court, 72–73
Indian Removal Act (1830), 43, 45
Indian Territory, 60, 74
Ishatai (prophet), 59–60, 63–64

Jerome Agreement, 73, 75–76
Jicarilla Apache, 39, 40
Jones, David E. (historian)
    accounts by, 17, 19, 21–22, 70–71

Kansas, 56, 57
Kansas River, 13, 44
Kiowa Apache, 42, 55, 60
Kotsoteka Comanches, 16, 19, 43

land
    diminished resources of, 46–47
    Jerome Agreement and, 73, 75–76
language, Comanche, 13, 18, 78, 81, 82
Lawton, Oklahoma, 16, 75, 82
legends, migration, 11–12
Lewis and Clark's expedition, 14
Lipan Apache, 39
Llano Estacado (Staked Plain), 8, 59
Louisiana Territory, 38, 40
Lucero, Juan, 42

Mackenzie, Colonel Randal, 60
maps
    bison range, 49
    Comanche Territory, 9
marriage and courtship, 30–32
meals, 35–36
meat, 35–36
medicine bag, 69
Medicine Lodge Treaty, 17, 57–58, 77, 81
medicine men (*puhakat*), 69–71
Mescalero Apache, 39

Mexico, 8, 39
migration, Comanche, 8, 10–12
missionaries, Christian, 70, 78
Missouri River, 8, 14, 15, 42
moccasins, 77
Montana, 10, 42
Mooney, James, 18–19, 76
Mowway (Kotsoteka chief), 43

Native American Church, 66, 78
Neeley, Bill, 67
New Mexico, 8, 10, 15, 24, 40
Nokoni Comanches, 16, 19
North American Indians (Catlin), 24
Noyes, Stanley (historian)
    accounts by, 28–29, 30, 40, 79–80
Nye, W. S., 61

Oklahoma, 46, 73, 78, 82
outposts, 40, 42, 46, 60

Padouca. *See* Comanche nation
Palo Duro Canyon, 60
Panhandle (Texas), 59
Parkeenaum Comanches, 15
Parker, Cynthia Ann, 59
peace pipe, 31, 53
Pecos Pueblo outpost, 40
Pecos River, 15, 19
pemmican, 36
Penetheka Comanches, 15, 16, 47, 55
peyote, 66, 78
pipe, tobacco, 31, 51
Platte River, 8
police force, 72
polygamy, 32
population, 82
Post Oak Jim (Comanche), 11
Potawatomie Indians, 44

Picture Credits

Cover Photo: Corbis/Bettmann
Archive Photos, 35, 51, 59, 74
Corbis, 17
Corbis/Bettmann, 81
Corbis/Eric Crighton, 36
Denver Public Library, 25, 33, 39, 54, 55, 63, 66, 77
Dover Publications, 64
FPG International, 52, 79
pixelpartners, 68
Library of Congress, 20, 29, 41, 44, 48, 57, 73, 75
Montana Historical Society, 13
North Wind Picture Archives, 18, 22, 27, 50
North Wind Pictures/N. Carter, 10

About the Author

Tom Streissguth has written more than 30 books of non-fiction for young readers, from *Life Among the Vikings* to *Utopian Visionaries; Lewis and Clark; Wounded Knee: The End of the Plains Indian Wars;* and the award-winning *Hustlers and Hoaxers*. He has written or collaborated on dozens of geography books as well as biographies and descriptive histories. His interests include music, languages, and travel. He has also co-founded a private language school, "Learn French!", which hosts summer tours each year in Europe. He lives in Florida with his wife and two daughters.